HEROES OF
THE FOURTH TURNING

"Rhetoric is both air raid siren and war cry in Will Arbery's Pulitzer Prize finalist . . . The strength of the show is how it breaks up the monolithic way the religious right is often portrayed."

—LILY JANIAK, *SAN FRANCISCO CHRONICLE*

"A must-see for liberals and conservatives alike . . . Of all the places I would have expected to hear 'Pat Buchanan's amazing!'—onstage in San Francisco was at the bottom of my list. But *Heroes of the Fourth Turning* is no ordinary play. It is a captivating, provocative piece of art you will thank yourself for seeing."

—BENJAMIN ESPOSITO, *STANFORD REVIEW*

"Art—visual, performance, or otherwise—can engage or repel, excite or anger, inspire or extinguish. Sometimes, it can do all these things, and more, all at once. Playwright Will Arbery achieves this in *Heroes of the Fourth Turning*, which uses a conversation among four friends as a lens to view conservative Catholicism and whiteness. Arbery grew up in this world and his sharp writing shows it."

—JACQUINN SINCLAIR, WBUR

"It does *Heroes of the Fourth Turning* a disservice to look at it only as a tool for understanding, or skewering, a certain group of people . . . to validate or advance a specific worldview isn't the play's intention. Instead, it gently and sometimes joltingly lets the characters lay out their constellation of individual beliefs on their own terms—beliefs about the world, about their place in it, about their faith, about their pain. But it's also interested in how the ideologies we cling to are often intrinsically linked to our personal pain, and often ineffective at helping us heal. Pain complicates belief."

—ALISSA WILKINSON, *VOX*

"You won't see the likes of Will Arbery's *Heroes of the Fourth Turning* come around that often—rigorous, haunting didactic on the religious right seen through the eyes of four young conservatives. Coming on the heels of Charlottesville and Trump, Arbery's cerebral script is both shocking and illuminating in its chilling portrayal of delusion and devotion in its extremes. Seen from the flip side of every liberal idea I call sacred, *Heroes* is a fascinating glimpse into the alarming dark underbelly that continues to lurk in the American psyche."

—STEVE MURRAY, *BROADWAY WORLD*

"Searing, vital, important . . . One of the best new plays to come down the pike in years. What could easily have been a bloviating political tirade against liberals becomes—with the aid of magical realism and the possibility that possession lurks within us all—a truly thoughtful dialogue of four soul-searching Christians. It is a miracle of Arbery's genius character sketches and relentless dialogue that we find ourselves sympathizing with these well-spoken young people."

—TONY FRANKEL, *STAGE AND CINEMA*

"A play about Catholic intellectuals debating the future of conservatism, *Heroes* aims at a much wider audience. Judging by the incredulous guffaws and gasps emanating from the house, it is clear that many are encountering these ideas for the very first time, and that makes this play thrilling. Arbery challenges us to look beyond our limited vantage point and wrestle with well-articulated counter perspectives. *Heroes of the Fourth Turning* is a tough watch, but it is absolutely necessary as America's competing tribes retreat into fortresses of affirmation."

—ZACHARY STEWART, *THEATERMANIA*

"Both sides are in their bubbles, the lack of interaction allows the mutual misunderstandings to fester and multiply, and social media makes the bifurcation so much worse. Shouldn't we make an effort to pop those bubbles, a little? *Heroes of the Fourth Turning* is a step toward increasing the dialogue. Thank you, Mr. Arbery. And playwrights of the right, if you're out there, let this be an incentive: With characters and arguments this compelling, you may actually get produced."

—MARC MILLER, *TALKIN' BROADWAY*

HEROES OF
THE FOURTH TURNING

Will Arbery

THEATRE COMMUNICATIONS GROUP / NEW YORK / 2023

The publication of *Heroes of the Fourth Turning* by Will Arbery, through TCG Books, is made possible with support by Mellon Foundation.

Special thanks to Judith O. Rubin for her generous support of this publication.

TCG books are exclusively distributed to the book trade by Consortium Book Sales and Distribution.

Library of Congress Control Numbers:
2022041403 (print) / 2022041404 (ebook)
ISBN 978-1-55936-988-6 (paperback) / ISBN 978-1-55936-943-5 (ebook)
A catalog record for this book is available from the Library of Congress.

Book design and composition by Lisa Govan
Cover design by Mark Melnick
Cover art: *The Unicorn Is in Captivity and No Longer Dead*, one of the series of seven tapestries comprising *The Hunt of the Unicorn*, c. 1495–1505. The Cloisters, Metropolitan Museum of Art, New York City.

First Edition, February 2023
Fourth Printing, February 2024

ACKNOWLEDGMENTS

Thank you to the entire staff at Playwrights Horizons, especially Lizzie Stern, Adam Greenfield, Ashley Chang, Billy McEntee, and Tim Sanford. In addition to my wonderful cast and creative team, additional thanks are due to Blake Zidell, Gigi Buffington, Ryan Kane, Madolyn Friedman, and Joan Sergay. And an extra thank you is due to Danya Taymor for her tireless leadership on—and radiant openness to—this play. You cannot fail with Danya by your side.

This play started as a short brunch play at EST/Youngblood, and grew into a full-length in that nurturing building. Thank you to Graeme Gillis and RJ Tolan, for creating the safest of spaces. And thank you to Linsay Firman, who had many long dramaturgical phone calls with me about the play, encouraging me through my early doubt. This play wouldn't exist without her. Thank you to Hal Brooks and The Cape Cod Theatre Project, providing us with a week of support which got this play to the finish line. Thank you to Vineyard Theatre and New York Theatre Workshop for their developmental support. Thank you to the actors who helped develop it, especially Drew

ACKNOWLEDGMENTS

Lewis, Will Dagger, Rachel Sachnoff, Keilly McQuail, Lydian Blossom, Blake DeLong, Sarah Tolan-Mee, Sofia Black-D'Elia, Colby Minifie, Gayle Rankin, Janet Zarish, Gabriel Ebert, and Damon Daunno. Thank you to Di Glazer, Sam Barickman, and Eva Dickerman.

Finally, this play was only possible because I grew up in the world it represents. It was born out of conversations with so many people, but thanks are due to Jason Kirstein, Trevor Lontine, and particularly Nathan Helms—whose spirit courses through every page of this play, and who was generous with notes on several drafts. And thank you, of course, to my parents, Glenn and Virginia Arbery, who never stop nudging me toward "that terrible beauty which sustains us." Thank you to all of my sisters, but most especially to Monica Arbery Corcoran, who, God help her, keeps letting me write about her. This play is dedicated to her, my hero.

HEROES OF
THE FOURTH TURNING

PRODUCTION HISTORY

Heroes of the Fourth Turning was developed by The Cape Cod Theatre Project (Hal Brooks, Artistic Director) in Falmouth, MA, in 2018.

Heroes of the Fourth Turning had its world premiere at Playwrights Horizons (Tim Sanford, Artistic Director; Leslie Marcus, Managing Director; Carol Fishman, General Manager) in New York City on October 7, 2019. It was directed by Danya Taymor. The scenic design was by Lael Jellinek, the costume design was by Sarafina Bush, the lighting design was by Isabella Byrd, the sound design was by Justin Ellington, and the fight direction was by J. David Brimmer; the voice and text coach was Gigi Buffington, and the production stage managers were Jenny Kennedy and Marisa Levy. The cast was:

JUSTIN	Jeb Kreager
EMILY	Julia McDermott
KEVIN	John Zdrojeski
TERESA	Zoë Winters
GINA	Michele Pawk

CHARACTERS

JUSTIN, male, thirty-eight
EMILY, female, twenty-five
KEVIN, male, twenty-eight
TERESA, female, twenty-nine
GINA, female, sixty-four

SETTING

A town of seven thousand in western Wyoming.
August 19, 2017.
Two days before the solar eclipse.
One week after the Charlottesville riot.
The night of Gina's inauguration as president of Transfiguration
    College of Wyoming.

How did I become a virus?
Hopelessness—
I feel the hopelessness.

—ANOHNI

And who among us is not neurotic, and has never complained that they are not understood? Why did you come here, to this place, if not in the hope of being understood, of being in some small way comprehended by your peers, and embraced by them in a fellowship of shared secrets? I don't know about you, but I just want to be held.

—MARY RUEFLE

FUGUE

1: a musical composition in which a theme is announced in one voice, imitated in succession by a fixed number of other voices, such as the soprano, alto, tenor, and bass, and interweaved contrapuntally until the climax.

2: a condition or phase involving the loss of recognition of one's own identity, often paired with sudden flight from one's home environment.

Justin's backyard in Lander, Wyoming. There's a concrete patio. There's a firepit with a few tree stumps around it for sitting. There's a lot of space.

It's early morning. Justin's sitting, drinking coffee. He might be praying. Then he sees something. He reaches behind him and grabs his rifle. He aims off.

He stays still for a very long time. Then he fires. Loud!

He goes off. Long pause, and then he returns with a deer corpse. A doe. He places it on a tarp by his porch. He goes inside his house.

We're alone with the deer.

He comes back out with a knife. He sits by the deer and looks at it.

He goes to gut it, but his hands start shaking. He tries again, his hands shake.

JUSTIN: Damn.

> *(He breathes. He goes to gut it.*
> *Now:*

It's night. Justin's dressed in nicer clothes. He's looking at the spot where he placed the deer. There's the noise of a party inside — about fifteen people. Most of them on their way out. We hear cars driving away staggered over the next few minutes.

Justin thinks he sees that he's stained his porch a bit with blood. He gets on his hands and knees and tries to clean the blood. Emily comes outside, walking with a cane. Justin stands up.)

EMILY: J?

JUSTIN: You okay?

EMILY: Yeah, just in a lot of pain. And people are stressing me out.

JUSTIN: Who's stressing you out?

EMILY: Just people. No sorry, everyone's lovely. Really, honestly—everyone's so *nice*. It's so stressful.

JUSTIN: I'll tell them to stop being so nice . . .

EMILY: No they're angels, *really*, I'm being a brat. It's cold out here why are you out here.

JUSTIN: Doesn't feel cold at all to me. Stomach? Head?

EMILY: Head, stomach. Heart beating fast. Panicky.

JUSTIN: Want me to take you home?

EMILY: I just saw myself in the mirror and I got so upset.

JUSTIN: Why?

EMILY: My belly. And my skin. I don't recognize myself.

JUSTIN: I think you look beautiful.

EMILY: You don't have to say that, that's not what I'm saying.

JUSTIN: Well.

(They both giggle. Emily shakes her head, doubles over in pain. Justin goes to her.)

Let me take you home.

EMILY: No, my mom's coming.

JUSTIN: I'll call her—I'll take you now.

EMILY: No, I need to try to be here. I need to try to be somewhere. I'm gonna get through this night. I'm gonna be

Ahh

Hm

Hm

Yep.

I'm gonna be present to this night. I'm not gonna turn away from it.

JUSTIN: I'm proud of you for even getting here.

EMILY: It'll probably make me bedridden for a month.

JUSTIN: Or maybe this is the first night of your healing.

EMILY: Stop it you'll make me cry. Okay it's cold I'm going inside.

JUSTIN: I got you.

(Justin supports her as they walk in.)

EMILY: "I got you." Doopy-doo.

JUSTIN: Doopy-doo. Yup.

EMILY: Simple as a doopy-doo.

JUSTIN: Just a simple hoopy-hoo.

EMILY: Yuppy-yoo.

(He walks her inside. They run into Kevin, who lights up a cigarette.)

KEVIN: Y'all okay?

EMILY: Yes

KEVIN: Sorry Emily I didn't mean to stress you out in there.

EMILY: You didn't

KEVIN: Okay

People are leaving

Everyone's so boring

EMILY: No they're wonderful

But I'm probably gonna leave

JUSTIN: Yeah I'm probably gonna need to sleep soon

KEVIN: Totally totally

I'm gonna smoke this then leave—

Oh my gosh the stars. The stars!

JUSTIN: Okay

(Justin closes the door.
Far away, the sound of gunshots.
Kevin has a bottle of whiskey. He wanders into the shadows.
He looks away from the stars. He laughs about something to
himself. We shouldn't be seeing this.)

KEVIN: no,

haha

something true:

this is something true:

this is something true:

(Kevin seems to freeze. Teresa comes outside.)

TERESA: Kevin.

KEVIN: Oh hey! What the heck, hey Teresa! Oh my gosh! You came!

TERESA: Are you leaving tomorrow?

KEVIN: Oh I dunno, I was maybe gonna stick around for the eclipse.

TERESA: Apologize.

KEVIN: When'd you get here? I thought you weren't gonna—

I was like "I guess she's not gonna—"

TERESA: Apologize.

KEVIN: For what

TERESA: For ignoring me at the ceremony.

KEVIN: I'm so sorry, Teresa. But I wasn't ignoring you . . .

TERESA: You were. All you gave me was a weak smile.

KEVIN: We were sitting far away from each other and then afterwards you were talking to all the professors . . .

TERESA: I beckoned you from across the tent.

KEVIN: I was just surprised to see you

TERESA: I was surprised to see *you*. You said "not attending" on Facebook.

KEVIN: Yeah I just—yeah. I didn't know if I would come but then on Thursday I realized that the school is in the Path of Totality so I was like ugh okay I wanna be in the Path of Totality, and the inauguration is right before, damn it's a sign, so I just got in my Camry and drove through the night. When'd you get here?

TERESA: Just now.

KEVIN: What time is it

TERESA: Almost eleven.

KEVIN: I think Emily is leaving and Justin wants to go to bed . . .

TERESA: No he said to stay and have a drink.

KEVIN: Oh rad. Okay rad. Where were you before

TERESA: I was trying to infiltrate the donor and board party.

KEVIN: Damn girl so Machiavellian

TERESA: Don't say that like it's a bad thing.

KEVIN: Sorry I'm so drunk

TERESA: No you're not.

KEVIN: No I had a million secret whiskeys, I'm an alcoholic probably but I'm sorry

TERESA: It's okay. I don't even care at all.

KEVIN: No listen Teresa I think there's a demon in me

I've been so so evil lately

I just say things to people, things just come out of my mouth

Like I'm just

AHHHH

AHHHHHHHH

I NEED TO CHANGE

SOMETHING NEEDS TO CHANGE IN ME
IT'S NOT OKAY
IT'S NOT OKAY

TERESA: Oh okay. I'm going back inside.

KEVIN: Teresa no, I'm so sorry, no! I'm the worst I'm the worst
I'm the worst

TERESA: It's nice to see that you still feel a weird responsibility
to perform your self-loathing for me. Goodnight, Kevin.

KEVIN: . . . I wasn't . . . performing my . . .

TERESA: You were. And listen, I like it. Wow I feel such déjà vu,
the big sky above us, you right in front of me, coiled up
with your dumb guilty face, it's one of my favorite shows.

KEVIN: You don't know me anymore, I've changed.

TERESA: You've *changed*?

KEVIN: Yeah I've changed.

TERESA: Okay. Let's do this. Let's catch up. Yeah?

KEVIN: Yeah!

TERESA: Tell me about your neighborhood.

KEVIN: Okay my neighb
Why

TERESA: Just tell me about your neighborhood.

KEVIN: Okay but . . . I really wasn't, wasn't *performing*, my,
Teresa—
Just cuz you say I was doing that doesn't mean it's true
that I was

TERESA: Just talk to me like an adult about adult things. Now.

KEVIN: Okay, fine.
All I do is come and cry.

TERESA: Stop it! Don't say gross things in a holy space.

KEVIN: This isn't a holy space it's just Justin's house

TERESA: The panopticon, Kevin, Catholicism is the panopticon.
This is a holy space.

KEVIN: It's also a profane space

TERESA: I asked about your NEIGHBORHOOD

KEVIN: OKAY. It's nice, I mean . . . It's Oklahoma so all the houses are small and flat

Like just sitting there just waiting to be ripped apart by a tornado

So I live in one of those

TERESA: Job?

KEVIN: Catholic textbooks company. It's horrible. I write about saints all day and then I come home and masturb— Whoop sorry.

TERESA: Stop.

KEVIN: Sorry God I'm sorry.

TERESA: Stop, it's me. Who do you live with?

KEVIN: With Jake Lopez my friend from home, you remember him? He visited a couple times, he went to Thomas Aquinas

TERESA: Sure yeah boring? Acne?

KEVIN: Yeah he works at the office with me. So we see each other all the time and barely know each other. And we go to Mass together three mornings a week ugh—

TERESA: Okay. Good job. Now ask me about mine.

KEVIN: Your what?

TERESA: Neighborhood.

KEVIN: Oh, how's your neighb—

TERESA: Glad you asked. It's in a part of Brooklyn called South Slope. It's right by a beautiful cemetery called Green Wood Cemetery, it's a national historic landmark. I need to tell this to Dr. Presson because she's in love with George Washington, so I live where the Battle of Brooklyn was fought in the Revolutionary War. George lost that battle, but escaped with his men, and they lived to fight on. The real heroes were the Maryland 400–400 men who sacrificed their lives, charging the British forces over and over and over, so that George and the revolutionaries could escape. So I feel the forces of heroic war when I walk outside, which I love. And Fiancé Patrick lives two avenues over.

KEVIN: Patrick yeah.

TERESA: There's a bakery nearby, so my neighborhood always smells like fresh bread. I love it. There are lots of babies. I live with an actress, someone I did plays with in high school. I was always the lead but anyway. She eats a lot of yogurt and talks to her mom every night. She's so boring.

KEVIN: Cool. How's your soul?

TERESA: Ugh, Kevin . . . I don't want to talk about my soul.

KEVIN: Why? Is it in peril?

TERESA: Is it in *peril*. Yeah probably! I do cocaine. I do too much cocaine.

KEVIN: Whoa

TERESA: Okay

KEVIN: WHOA

TERESA: Okay okay

KEVIN: What's it like

TERESA: It's fucking great, just do it, it was made for you.

KEVIN: Whoa

Okay you know what

Okay I will

Okay I'm ready

Do you have some

TERESA: And I'm a gossip and I'm embarrassingly ambitious and I haven't talked to my weird sad mother in months even though she's like a forty-five-minute train ride away . . .

KEVIN: Still in Connecticut?

TERESA: Yeah and when I see her I can barely look at her, I act like she's diseased because she is.

KEVIN: What's diseased about her?

TERESA: She's weak, she's . . .

Okay, no more soul stuff.

KEVIN: Come on

TERESA: I just want to have a normal conversation like adults.

KEVIN: I think talking about our souls being in peril is a very adult conversation

TERESA: You're so boring

KEVIN: Have you lost Christ

TERESA: No.

KEVIN: Are you so New York now

TERESA: Maybe.

KEVIN: Did you have sex again

TERESA: No, stop, no.

KEVIN: Did you become a liberal

TERESA: I'm more conservative than ever, Kevin. I'm the poster boy.

KEVIN: Right I mean that's your *brand*, but . . .

TERESA: No. To the core.

KEVIN: Rad, that's rad.

TERESA: Ugh never say "rad" to me again.

KEVIN: Okay got it. Well let me tell you about *my* soul.

TERESA: No thank you.

KEVIN: I've been so curious and terrified about—

TERESA: No, I said no. I'm just not in the mood. It's too overwhelming. Sorry.

KEVIN: Oh. Um, okay.

(He almost gets sad, but fights it off.)

What we need to do is have a big conversation . . . !
What we need to do is have a big conversation . . . !
Like we used to do
With our feet in the pool
Having big conversations with our feet in the pool is one of my favorite things in this life

TERESA: Whenever we, ugh.

KEVIN: Tell me

TERESA: No.

KEVIN: Tell me

TERESA: Whenever we have a big conversation, it's really nice for a while, but it always ends with you saying you should become a priest, and then crying about how you'd be a bad priest, and then crying about how much you want a girlfriend.

KEVIN: Oh, haha, yeah, haha, I won't do any of that. Let's pretend we're not at Justin's, but rather at the pool. You want it, I see it in your eyes. You've been waiting for this, you haven't had a big conversation in so long

TERESA: My job is to have big conversations.

KEVIN: But that's your *job*! You work too hard and you're always "on" and now you're ready to just talk and be so so human with your friend

Okay here's my thing:

Here's my thing for the big conversation:

I've been holding on to this:

It's so messed up:

It'll lead to a four-hour conversation:

Okay: okay:

Why the heck do we have to love the Virgin Mary?

TERESA: No.

KEVIN: I'm serious. Why Mary? What does she have to do with our salvation?

Who the heck *is* this woman?

Why do I have to love this *mom*?

TERESA: . . . are you even still a Catholic?

KEVIN: Just let me ask the question! I just don't get it. I get that she gave birth to Jesus and that she had no sin but when I think of her I don't *feel* anything . . .

TERESA: This is always your thing. I can't make you feel the feelings, Kevin! I can help you think the thoughts but I can't make you feel the feelings. That is impossible. Okay?

If you're not feeling it, you're not feeling it, and that ain't on me. God, Kevin—*evolve*. Why did I come here?

KEVIN: Because Dr. Presson is coming

TERESA: Jim or Gina or both

KEVIN: Gina

TERESA: But is she *really*? When?

KEVIN: Uh

TERESA: When is she coming?

KEVIN: Soon soon so soon she's coming she's picking Emily up

TERESA: When though when.

KEVIN: Soon!

TERESA: Okay

KEVIN: So help me with this Mary thing . . . help me *think* the thoughts, that's fine.

Why do I feel . . . why do you *think* I feel anger against the blessed blessed Virgin Mary? Please Teresa please I won't be annoying I just love being around your brain, this is so rare—

TERESA: AHHH OKAY

Let me

(She looks down and thinks.)

You're afraid of the scandal of the particular.

KEVIN: Oh!

What is that.

TERESA: This is the thing about God. He makes us work out our salvation through other people.

KEVIN: Ah, why

TERESA: It's just how He works. It's the whole way the Bible is structured—the ladder of revelation. The way God reveals himself to ordinary people. When they receive the Word, common people like Abraham and Mary are worried that they won't be believed by people like you—who sit there thinking, what's so special about *that* person? Why should God choose *them*? Walter Brueggemann said

KEVIN: Who

TERESA: Brueggemann. Brueggemann.

KEVIN: I don't know who that is

TERESA: Yeah but I *do* and he said—

KEVIN: Wait isn't he Protestant?

TERESA: We're allowed to read Protestants idiot, Dr. Jim gave me the book okay?, he thought I could handle it, LISTEN, Brueggemann said that every single revelation in the Bible is evidence of the scandal of the particular. The scandal of this particular person getting this particular revelation. This carpenter, this shepherd, this stutterer, this virgin. And *grace*—grace always accompanying the grotesque. Sometimes the moments that are the most grotesque are the closest to transcendent grace.

KEVIN: I

TERESA: I mean think about it politically: we almost had a president who was the opposite of the Virgin Mary in every sense. A woman who had scrubbed her image clean of any particularity, any humanity, any grace. A woman who was at the forefront of the effort to neuter all particularity. An effort to silence religion, mystery, and morality entirely. Somehow, thank God, we elected the more human and particular of the two options. Actually this is at the heart of my writing right now. The nation as the last bastion of the particular. The kingdom is the kingdom and the kingdom has particular laws. The lepers need to be *healed*, not championed for their leprosy. We're not meant to structure our society according to every freakish chosen "right." We're supposed to strive for the good. The particular, written, incarnate, natural Christian good. Otherwise, what are we? A throbbing mass of genderless narcissists. There's no "thisness" in the liberal future. There's no *there* there. It's empty. What's really radical is *sacrifice*. Painful particularity is what we need. Otherwise we're culturally lobotomized. We'll be force-fed brand-new oppressed identities every year and we'll bow to the tyranny of rights. Fuck rights. Europe right now has no idea what to do with Islam. It's going to eat them alive because it's so fucking specific and there's a *power* there. We need to embrace our American identity as a representative of Christ on the globe. Because it's Christianity alone that has a God who knows what it is to be a *man*, who sacrificed his life as a *man*, who felt the full pain of our particular human journey into death. And we need to be ready to sacrifice ourselves the way he sacrificed himself for all of us. What a scandal! What a scandal that we would rather put up a wall, that we would rather *die*, than be subsumed by an invading disease. What a scandal that each one of us confused, fragile, ordinary people is called to this sacrifice. And what a fucking scandal that the God who created the skies and the leviathans would care about one particular person, one particular *woman*, so much so that he would give her the son of God, so much so that he would become a particular person himself. So yeah, that's why you're afraid of Mary. She's so ordinary. Boom. Struggle with that, fall in love with that, and eat it.

(Teresa slaps a mosquito on her arm. Kevin is sad.)

What, Kevin. Are you okay?
KEVIN: Yes, it's just
    I got sad
    If you're all about the particular, and ordinary people
    Then why don't you want to hear about all my things
    My particular things

TERESA: . . . What? I asked you about your neighborhood.

KEVIN: But my confused and fragile things, my soul things, my
ordinary soul things
And not just tonight—like *ever*—like when I reach out
to you, just to talk . . . why do you always shut me down?

TERESA: Honestly?
Because you're weak.
And it disgusts me.

(Pause.)

KEVIN: But that's what I love about Catholicism:
It lets me be weak.

TERESA: Yeah I don't know. Sorry. I'm awful. I am, I am sorry.
I just.
I just wish you'd grow into yourself a little more. Be a bit
more of a man.

KEVIN *(Hiding his face)*: You think I'm a little boy

TERESA: No, I don't. I think you're stuck.

KEVIN: I know that I'm stuck but—

TERESA: I think you blame your problems on demons, but really
you're just morally lazy.

KEVIN: Okay I'm sorry—I won't talk about anything anymore.
It's just I wanted to have a big conversation, and you just said
everything. You had the whole conversation by yourself.

TERESA: Oh I'm sorry did you want to *contribute* more? You're
not actually a good conversationalist, Kevin. You make
everything about yourself, Kevin. Good conversations ele-
vate the conversants. You, without fail, bring it back down
to your own shit.

KEVIN: Teresa I just
I just need to say, don't get mad
I just want a
I want a girlfriend.

I'm not crying about it, I'm just saying. I want a girlfriend.
I think it would make me better
It would make me a good conversationalist
I'm so alone all the time, I forgot how to talk to people
I spend so much time online, I'm addicted to it, I'm sick
And I need a girlfriend.

TERESA: Yeah, you do. You do. You absolutely do. But it's not gonna be me.

KEVIN: I didn't say I wanted it to be you! You're engaged.

TERESA: Yes I'm engaged. To a man among men.

KEVIN: I can't wait for the wedding

TERESA: Oh right I invited you. You're gonna have a huge crush on Patrick.

KEVIN: I'm not gonna have a crush on your husband, what the heck

TERESA: You will—he's everything you want to be. So funny. Complex but cocksure. He's Connecticut like me. I always needed a Connecticut, ultimately, I think. Delicious.

KEVIN: Ew

TERESA: And it's not gonna be Emily either.

KEVIN: What

TERESA: Emily can't love you either—women want to feel like they have the power to melt a rock and if you're never a rock then how can they melt the rock.

KEVIN: I don't understand anything you're saying

TERESA: I'm sorry this sucked. Sorry. Sorry. I've stopped being able to lie. Don't tear yourself apart over this. There's a war coming, dude.

KEVIN: What

TERESA: There's a war coming. And I want you to be on the right side. I want you to be strong enough to fight. Remember your roots. You went to a school where you got wilderness training, where you spoke conversational Latin and locked your phone in a safe for four years and rode horses and built igloos and memorized poems while scaling mountains, and you were strong and you were one of us, and now look at you, you're a pale American soy boy.

KEVIN: A pale what

TERESA: Just make a decision not to be weak anymore, and stick to it. Just promise yourself that you'll never do this again. It doesn't matter that I'm your old friend. I am a beautiful grown woman standing in front of you. When you have a beautiful grown woman standing in front of you, you'll listen to her, you'll talk to her about normal boring adult things, and the whole time you'll be ready to snap a neck if someone attacks her. And if you move into a big conversation, you won't pull it down into your fucking shame. Never do this again. Never pull things down into your shame. There's no more shame, Kevin. No more shame. Not from us. Not from our side. It's slowing us down. Stop slowing us down.

KEVIN: . . . a war?

(Emily and Justin come outside.)

EMILY: Hey Teresa! You came!

TERESA: Yes. Hi again. Is um—is your mom coming?

EMILY: She better be. I need to sleep, I'm so exhausted.

TERESA: Okay yay. Okay yay. Whaddup y'all?

JUSTIN: Can I get y'all anything to drink

EMILY: Aren't y'all cold out here

TERESA: No it's not cold

KEVIN: Does anyone want to see the eclipse with me, we're in the Path of Totality

EMILY: Oh um Justin wants to play a song.

JUSTIN: No *you* want me to play a song

EMILY: Who wants to hear it

TERESA: Oh. I do. Justin's voice makes me . . .

KEVIN: What kind of a song

JUSTIN: Outsider-country I suppose. Townes.

KEVIN: Okay a song

EMILY: Are y'all okay

TERESA: Yeah we're fine.

KEVIN *(To Teresa)*: A war?

TERESA: Shut up.

EMILY *(To Kevin)*: Are you okay

KEVIN: Mhm

(Kevin drinks some whiskey.)

TERESA: Okay, give me some of that.

(She takes the whiskey bottle and drinks some. She gives it back to Kevin.)

Okay, play your song, Justin.

JUSTIN: Alright. Sorry if I'm a little rusty

EMILY: Shh, play

(Justin plays "Nothin'" by Townes Van Zandt.)

JUSTIN:

Hey mama, when you leave
Don't leave a thing behind
I don't want nothin'
I can't use nothin'

Take care into the hall
And if you see my friends
Tell them I'm fine
Not using nothin'

Almost burned out my eyes
Threw my ears down to the floor
I didn't see nothin'
I didn't hear—

(Suddenly, there's a horrible screech. It's so loud. Part machine, part animal. It overwhelms the stage. Everyone covers their ears.)

TERESA: What the—
EMILY: OH MY GOD
KEVIN: WOW
JUSTIN: Geez
EMILY: WHAT IS THAT

(It dies down.)

What was that?
JUSTIN: Uh, that's my generator. Sorry guys. Sometimes it, uh. Be right back.

(He leaves.)

EMILY: Oh my Lord
KEVIN: Teresa, a war?
TERESA: *Is* Dr. Gina coming?
EMILY: Yes dear.
TERESA: When?
EMILY: In ten minutes I think. Less.
TERESA: Actually though?
EMILY: Six minutes ago she texted me that she was leaving Dr. Poponcini's . . .
TERESA: Oh my God, okay. I'll stay. Yes, Kevin, a war. Let me go wash my face. It's so dry here. I forgot how dry it was here. I'm so ugly. Do you think Justin has any Kiehl's?

(Teresa laughs and leaves.)

KEVIN: hey i'm sorry again for being intense in there, about the
    deer ticks, i wasn't thinking
EMILY: it's fine
KEVIN: how are you feeling do you need anything
EMILY: fine stop
    don't
KEVIN: what
EMILY: i just i really don't, i don't want to talk about my *health*
KEVIN: okay
EMILY: thanks

(Pause.)

KEVIN: You know who's intense?
EMILY: Who?
KEVIN: Teresa.
EMILY: She's *so* intense. What'd she do?
KEVIN: Oh you know, talked to me about cocaine and sex and
    war.
EMILY: Oh gosh. What did she say about cocaine and sex?
KEVIN: I mean, you know she had sex, right? While she was here?
    She almost got kicked out. But she was granted clemency.
EMILY: Seriously?
KEVIN: Yeah.
EMILY: No way. Who'd she have sex with?
KEVIN: Ah
    Never mind
EMILY: You can't do that
    Tell me
KEVIN: No I um
EMILY: Yes say it.
KEVIN: No Emily look at me seriously:
    No.
EMILY: AHHH

KEVIN: I really really just totally can't. She swore me to secrecy.
Okay?

EMILY: Oh . . .

(Pause.)

Was it

KEVIN: What

EMILY: Nothing

Never mind

Sorry I asked

KEVIN: No I'm sorry.

EMILY: Wow, she is . . . I'm sorry but she is such a hypocrite. At
the ceremony, she had a little audience and she was trying
to get me to admit that my liberal friend was a bad person.
And I'm sorry, but I think it's unfair to argue that I should
cut ties with someone just because they're on the other side.
I can't see things in black-and-white like that. I have a full
faith, it's my rock, it's my pain, it's my everything—and
I also am friends with whoever I want to be friends with. It
doesn't change the faith at all. It doesn't change my love for
God, or my love for Jesus.

KEVIN: Oh God

EMILY: What

KEVIN: You're just very compelling and nice. *And* you're sick.
How do you do it

EMILY: I just do it like my gal Flannery O: "Give me the courage
to stand the pain to get the grace."

KEVIN: Yeah. I know you see the grace in everything.

EMILY: Not in *everything*.

KEVIN: Okay, not in everything.

EMILY: There's so much pain. And there's so much *time*. So
much time of me just sitting in my pain. And I get so angry.
I get so small. I want to die. I want to die *a lot*. And that's

as graceless as you can get, believe me. It's . . . nuh-uh. It's
really, really ugly, and it just . . . and I, anyway . . . sorry! . . .

KEVIN: No it's okay. Gosh Emily, I didn't know.

EMILY: Whatever it's just the disease. It's just the bug eating
my brain. But we all have that inside of us. We all have a
labyrinth in there and it's just you and the Trinity, trying to
find the way out.

KEVIN: oh God yeah you're right i'm not

    doing it right

    idiot idiot

EMILY: Doing what right?

KEVIN: Any of it. I'm empty.

EMILY: No you're not. What are you talking about?

KEVIN: I just am. When I think of the Eucharist . . . when I think
of what we *actually* believe that to be? We are talking about
the murder of our God—we're witnesses, every *day*, to the
sacrifice He made for us, with His physical body. We're
talking about His blood, His wounds, and we are proclaim-
ing His *mangled body* to be *in the room* with us. And then we
eat Him and He literally becomes part of our *cellular body*.
How are we not falling down on the ground and WEEP-
ING—every time? Why am I ever bored? Just waiting to
get out and have *brunch*? Because it's been two thousand
years and we know the story already? But the story is new
every time because there are new kinds of sinning every
day—and He dies for those sins, every time, every day, all
over the world, in every church. He is dying He is dying
He is dying, He is giving us His body so that we can LIVE,
and meanwhile I'm just sneakily checking my phone and
speed-praying by rote, just saying the words. I never *feel*
anything . . . and I definitely don't think in those terms . . .
the labyrinth, the grace . . .

EMILY: Why should you think in those terms? Those are my
terms, don't take 'em.

KEVIN: A maze, a maze sounds fun, instead of this emptiness—
EMILY: Emptiness is beautiful!

It's all beautiful.

I don't know. Please, can we just—

Every second we're not destroying something, destroying someone, destroying the world, destroying ourselves—every second we're creating and coexisting instead of tearing this place apart—I just think it's miraculous.

(Perhaps now we realize that Justin has been listening in the shadows.)

KEVIN: but see

but emily

sometimes i want to destroy
EMILY: You do?
KEVIN: Yes—yeah. It's the only thing I can get to, in my brain: gather everyone in a place, the entirety of the secular world, all their phones and porn and astrology and orgies, and then blow it up, as though destroying will let truth rise out of that—something solid and undeniable will emerge for us then, and we can look at it with our eyes, and know it to be true.
EMILY: Yeah whoa

Your labyrinth is not my labyrinth.
KEVIN: You think I'm horrible.
EMILY: No. I think you're suffering. Ain't we all, Kev Kev . . .
KEVIN: haha
EMILY: Kev Kev
KEVIN: haha
EMILY: Ah whatever. It's all impossible.
KEVIN: Yeah. I thank God.
EMILY: You thank God?

KEVIN: I thank God. I thank God that it's impossible. I thank God that I'm not just a boring Catholic Hufflepuff foot soldier. I thank God that you've stayed in touch with me. I thank God for Facebook Messenger. I think you're the most amazing human being I've ever met. And I'm so grateful and I thank God.

EMILY: Oh. Kevin, jeesh . . .

KEVIN: Do you wanna go see the eclipse with me on Monday?

JUSTIN *(From behind them)*: Did I tell y'all the story about the grateful acre?

EMILY: Ah!

KEVIN: Whoa how long have you been there?

JUSTIN: Just a minute. Yeah, uh . . . that generator's messed up. Sorry about that y'all.

(He pours himself some whiskey.)

EMILY: What did you say about a story? What story?

JUSTIN: About the grateful acre.

EMILY: What's the story about the grateful acre?

JUSTIN: It's a story I made up. I want to make it into a children's book or something.

EMILY: Are you kidding me right now?

JUSTIN: No, why.

EMILY: That's just the most beautiful thing I've ever heard. You're writing a children's book? Oh my sweet Lord. Please tell me about the grateful acre.

JUSTIN: Okay. The grateful acre was created when God created the Earth. The grateful acre was grateful to wake up one day and realize that it was an acre. God smiled upon it and the grateful acre was grateful. It was grateful when dirt appeared upon it. Even though the dirt made the acre feel heavier, the acre was grateful. It was grateful when grass appeared upon it. Even though the grass ate the dirt and made the acre feel smaller, the acre was grateful. It was grateful when insects crawled inside it. Even though the insects ate the grass which ate the dirt, the acre felt grateful. It was grateful when the beasts walked upon it. Even though the beasts trampled on the grass and ate the insects, the acre felt grateful. It was grateful when man stepped upon it. Even though man killed the grass and ate the beasts and insects and polluted the dirt, the acre felt grateful. It was grateful when man built upon it. Even when the grass disappeared and the dirt disappeared and the acre was poured upon with concrete, and a tower rose upon it, and the acre sunk deeper into the earth, the acre was grateful. When the building fell, the acre was grateful. Even though the acre was covered in stone and plastic and death, the acre was grateful. When the air filled with radiation, the acre was grateful. When the acre stopped being able to breathe, the acre was grateful. When the acre slipped into a coma, the acre was grateful.

For ten thousand centuries of silence, the acre was grateful.

And when the acre woke up, its first thought was: "I am grateful."

And when the grass came back, the acre was grateful.

And when the bugs came back, the acre was grateful.

And when the beasts came back, the acre was grateful.

And the acre was grateful.

And the acre was grateful.

And the acre waited for man to come back.

And when man never came back, the acre was grateful.

(Pause.)

The end.

EMILY: Oh my Sweet Lord Jesus Christ
    You made that up?
JUSTIN: Yup.
EMILY: Oh my Sweet Jesus God and Lord
KEVIN: Yeah that was cool Justin
EMILY: Oh my gosh
    Oh my sweet Jesus gosh
    Oh I could just

(They all look at the sky.)

Oh my Lord and Gosh
JUSTIN: Haha
EMILY: My boys!
JUSTIN: "Boys."
EMILY: My men.
KEVIN: Yeah this feels good this feels nice. This sky. Oh my gosh.
    "Per aspera ad astra." Yeah. "Per aspera ad astra."
EMILY: What is that?
KEVIN: Latin.
EMILY: I know but
KEVIN: "Through suffering to the stars."

(They look at the stars for a long beat.)

I miss Wyoming
EMILY: I miss Wyoming even when I'm in it
JUSTIN: Whoa that gave me a chill.
EMILY: Haha really
JUSTIN: Yeah let's not talk about— Damn.
EMILY: What
JUSTIN: It's just, uh. It's like my story. Everything's disappearing.
EMILY: What's disappearing J?
JUSTIN: All the good old things and ways.

EMILY *(Imitating his accent)*: "All the good old things and ways."

(Kevin laughs. Emily laughs.)

No but what, J?

JUSTIN: Nothing. Nothing.

EMILY: "Whoa that gave me a chill."

KEVIN: "Whoa that gave me a chill."

JUSTIN: I won't speak anymore.

EMILY: J, say it

JUSTIN: Do y'all notice blood on the porch here

EMILY: What?

JUSTIN: Never mind, it was a deer. I shot it and felt, I felt weird after—I've never felt so weird after, before.

EMILY: Do you want to talk about it?

JUSTIN: Nah. Was trying to gut it. My hands were shaking.

EMILY: You're so good.

KEVIN *(Mocking Justin's accent)*: "And when man killed a deer upon it, the acre was grateful."

Justin uh what do you think is changing?

JUSTIN: It's just becoming harder and harder to hold on to what's good. I'm talking eudaemonia. I'm talking The Good.

KEVIN: Really, Justin?

JUSTIN: What

KEVIN: Aristotle? Evolve.

JUSTIN: Heh

EMILY: Evolve how

KEVIN: Plato, Plato

EMILY: Oh

JUSTIN: Even though Plato came first

EMILY: Evolve backwards

KEVIN: All the best things came first

Nothing good has ever been new

EMILY: What

KEVIN: I'm just saying words

JUSTIN *(To Emily)*: I was talking this out with your parents.

EMILY: Ughh they're so annoying

KEVIN: *What?*

EMILY: They're all college all the time, can we not talk about the college please

KEVIN: Your parents are amazing, Emily. Gina and Jim!

EMILY: Okay.

KEVIN: Emily do you wish you'd gone to this school?

EMILY: Not at all

I had to get away from them

KEVIN: But like, this is the best curriculum

JUSTIN: It really is

And it really is because of them

They feel the urgency, the urgency of

EMILY: I know.

JUSTIN: The *return* to

EMILY: Yes. It's very urgent. Much more urgent than my nonstop pain and confusion.

KEVIN: Yeah but look Emily I mean your parents are trying to like save the country basically. Like they're basically the opposite of *The Benedict Option*—they're going into the world rather than retreating—

JUSTIN: Oh I like *The Benedict Option*.

EMILY: What is that?

KEVIN: A book that says we're not gonna win this thing and we should just retreat.

JUSTIN: No that's an oversimplification.

KEVIN: Whatever it's so spineless.

JUSTIN: You don't think Transfiguration College of Wyoming is the epitome of *The Benedict Option*?

KEVIN: What?

JUSTIN: Smack dab in the middle of the least populated state in the union, six hours from the nearest urban area. Our school didn't accept federal funding.

KEVIN: Okay well maybe this is my point, then: the school's explicit mission was to train me to be a leader *in the world*, but I was *not* ready for the world. It's been seven years and this whole time I've been paralyzed. What have I *done* with all of it? Maybe I need to get spanked around a little bit. Maybe I need to move to New York like Teresa did and just like, *dive in.*

JUSTIN: No.

KEVIN: What

JUSTIN: Stay away from New York. Deepen your spiritual life, and get away from urban temptations.

KEVIN: Maybe what I need is more urban temptations.

JUSTIN: What?

KEVIN: Maybe repression makes me a worse person.

JUSTIN: No sir.

KEVIN: Maybe I need to be in the den of lions, in order to really be the Catholic I was meant to be. Like there are some priests, like Jesuits, who thrive in that kind of environment. Ugh do I need to be a priest?

JUSTIN: Maybe. But I don't know if you need to do that in a den of lions.

KEVIN: Why?

JUSTIN: Well, as one example . . . cities are obviously hubs of LGBT activity, and I don't think it's healthy to be around LGBT activity.

KEVIN: Why—do you think I'd become gay?

JUSTIN: I just think proximity to LGBT is a threat to Christian children and families. Exposure makes you porous to infection. And all this babble about gender being fluid and nonbinary. We are living in barbaric times.

KEVIN: But why can't we meet it, engage with it—

JUSTIN: Because it's hard to confront people who you know won't change.

KEVIN: What's wrong with it being hard? It should be hard.

JUSTIN: And all the power is on their side. All the bureaucracy, and soon—all the laws. Everyone working for any business or public school will be frog-marched through diversity-and-inclusion training. It won't just be about *tolerating*, which we *do*, it will be about *affirming* their disorder. Which is a sin.

KEVIN: I don't disagree. So what do you propose?

JUSTIN: Stay among the like-minded.

KEVIN: You want us to just become a quivering bubble of Christian cowards?

JUSTIN: Wow. No. I want us to put our heads down, preserve our culture, and wait for the hedonists to eat themselves alive.

KEVIN: Well maybe I want to save some of the hedonists.

EMILY: Mmm. Kev, you're so good.

JUSTIN: Yeah that's fair.

KEVIN: Like what if the way is be the holy fool? To get in there, to meld, to fuse, to engage, to dance and laugh together on the street. To live our truth, in the face of theirs. To let two competing facts exist in the same space. To imagine a Heaven we can all graduate into.

EMILY: Wow Kev that was beautiful.

KEVIN: Yeah that was beautiful! I'm on a roll!

(Kevin takes a huge swig of whiskey.)

EMILY: J it honestly reminds me of the grateful acre.

JUSTIN: Oh yeah?

EMILY: Yes, being grateful for whatever tramples you . . . but isn't that so hard?

JUSTIN: It is hard, yeah.

KEVIN *(After a burp)*: No it's not as simple as the grateful acre.

JUSTIN: The acre is essentially a sponge, retaining and absorbing the foreign elements which infiltrate it. But it cannot be erased of its essential *this*ness, which is that of an acre.

EMILY: Mmmmmmm

KEVIN: Can I talk!

EMILY: Kev, I'm sorry.

KEVIN: Yeah I can't . . . I can't with this grateful acre. This is why I hate Facebook, I can't—

People get obsessed with basic-ass *memes* and they're not actually engaging with the complexity of these . . .

EMILY: The grateful acre is not basic-ass.

KEVIN: Okay SORRY Justin I didn't mean to offend you.

JUSTIN: You didn't.

KEVIN: This is the same problem as Facebook yeah DAMN I keep getting into these little arguments and offending people. The comments wars—

Because it's *hard* to be the holy fool—it's hard to dance with the devil.

And I try to engage with this transgender thing and everyone *IMMEDIATELY* shuts me down and it's like okay do you *want* me to hate you?

EMILY: Oh man what

KEVIN: What

EMILY: Can we not with the transgender bashing, can we not

KEVIN: Sorry, whoa, I wasn't *bashing*. Damn, you're mad at me

EMILY: No no! Sorry I just don't want things to become hateful.

KEVIN: Oh my gosh—you think I'm hateful. I can't believe you think that about me. I'm—whoa.

EMILY: No, Kev Kev . . . I'm sorry. I did *not* mean that you were hateful. Not at all.

KEVIN: Okay. I just thought I was talking about *engaging* with them, and like, Justin's the one calling them *barbarians* . . .

EMILY: You are so good. Please speak.

KEVIN: No I just

EMILY: I'm sorry

KEVIN: No I just—yeah, they're not even inviting us to this conversation. It's this insane thing that they're all getting hung up on, this small minority of confused people, but all the people all the people like *suddenly* so defensive about using the word "they" but "they" doesn't make any damn grammatical sense. Whoa Justin I just noticed that you are packing a pistol, can I see it

JUSTIN: No

KEVIN: Right

EMILY: Guys guess what I hate guns.

KEVIN: Justin is a person you trust with a gun, Emily, he was a freakin sharpshooter in the *Marines*, Emily!

EMILY: "He was a freakin sharpshooter in the Marines, Emily"

KEVIN: Hahaha no but he's . . . hey Justin: You have killed people.

JUSTIN *(After a beat)*: It's fascinating the transgender thing

KEVIN: It's a transgender world and I'm a transgender uh

And how do we

Like if I'm dancing with them

Like do I dance them to the gates of hell and slam the gate shut behind them

EMILY: Whoa, Kevin, please . . .

KEVIN: Sorry whoa guys I don't know anything about anything.

EMILY: I want to say: begotten not made. For me it's just that. Begotten not made. We are *given* our*selves*. There's a mystery in the givenness. And we're sharing that givenness with God. And I don't judge them, and I'm not saying they're bad people at *all*. But I do feel these days that it's like . . . it's like it's popular to reject the truth of our*selve*s as *given*.

KEVIN: You sound like your mom

EMILY: Ugh

KEVIN: In a good way

JUSTIN: Your dad was saying and I thought it was brilliant that it's this Cartesian "neo-Gnosticism" that convinces people

that their souls are somehow separate from their bodies,
and their bodies can somehow be fashioned however they
like.

EMILY: Oh that's beautiful J, that's so—my body is so much a
part of me I can't even begin

> And I didn't choose this, my body is just a friggin
> prairie of pain,
> and I can't choose to make it go away
> It's just what I've been given.

KEVIN: A prairie of pain. Oh Emily, I want you to know that
you're going to be okay

EMILY: Yes I know

> For seven years, I've been "going to be okay"
> Do you mind if we say the rosary? Or just start one?

JUSTIN: Sure

EMILY: Is that weird, we don't have to

KEVIN: No let's do it

EMILY *(Getting out her rosary)*: I want to say this for

KEVIN: Hold on, hold on one sec. I just have to

> Real fast.
> The thing about me and whiskey

*(He starts to go off to pee, but then suddenly turns around, and
with too much fervor, and very fast, recites some motherfucking
William Wordsworth.)*

> The world is too much with us; late and soon,
> Getting and spending, we lay waste our powers;—
> Little we see in Nature that is ours;
> We have given our hearts away, a sordid boon!
> This Sea that bares her bosom to the moon;
> The winds that will be howling at all hours,
> And are up-gathered now like sleeping flowers;
> For this, for everything, we are out of tune;

It moves us not. Great God! I'd rather be
A Pagan suckled in a creed outworn;
So might I, standing on this pleasant lea,
Have glimpses that would make me less forlorn;
Have sight of Proteus rising from the sea;
Or hear old Triton blow his wreathèd horn.

EMILY: Mmm.

KEVIN: I gotta pee so bad.

(He goes off to pee. Emily and Justin look at each other and laugh.)

EMILY: *So* proud of himself . . .

(They laugh. They look at the sky.)

Hey does this school actually . . . make good people?

JUSTIN: Yes. I think it attracts good people and makes them better.

EMILY: But doesn't it seem like Kevin is so wildly confused
And Teresa seems so cold . . . like she's switched off a part of herself.

JUSTIN: Yeah.

EMILY: I thought this would just be a nice party celebrating my mom

JUSTIN: It was

EMILY: But everyone's being so weird

JUSTIN: Yeah. But everyone else left. And everyone else is pretty great. I felt so heartened tonight seeing how everyone's ended up. Healthy. Happy. Humble. Building families. This school makes ninety-nine-percent *great* people. So that feeling you're feeling might just be because of Kevin and Teresa. Specifically. As people.

EMILY *(Laughing)*: Are they the weird lingerers? Are we left with the weird lingerers?

JUSTIN: Haha yes they *are* the weird lingerers

EMILY: Hahaha

Did you know Teresa almost got kicked out when she was a student? For having sex?

JUSTIN: I think I did know that yeah

Yeah small school, word spreads

EMILY: Why did she not get kicked out?

JUSTIN: She's savvy

EMILY: What a sad savvy woman

Oh man J I need a buddy

Are you my buddy?

JUSTIN: Looks that way.

EMILY: Where should we watch the eclipse on Monday?

JUSTIN: I know a spot. Up by Crowheart.

EMILY: I'm so excited.

(She gasps.)

J, I got so, I got *angry* this morning. I couldn't lift my head and I just lay there like

F this F this F this F this

Just F this

Just faaaaarck this

Just over and over.

I was mad at God.

And I could feel Him, just sitting there and just taking it.

JUSTIN: You think it's bad to get mad like that, but it ain't.

EMILY: "But it ain't." Hahahaha you did that one on purpose, you play into it so hard

JUSTIN: No I do not.

EMILY: "No I do not."

JUSTIN: Well

EMILY: No, I know. And thank you, I know.

JUSTIN: Okay because I think of the agony and the ecstasy, right?
And what does it matter, if you're *feeling* it?
If you're feeling it, you're one of the lucky ones.

EMILY: Hm. I don't know.

JUSTIN: You don't know?

EMILY: I do not know. I do not know about *feeling it*. I think feeling it might just be dangerous. It makes me feel violated. Taken over. I think it might just make me a non-person.

JUSTIN: You're not a non-person

EMILY: If you say so.

Okay okay. Everything will be okay. Haha. I'll just, I'll just wake up one day and I'll be like, *whoa, I'm a real woman.* I can move through the world as a woman, and love as a woman. And you'll

JUSTIN: I'll what?

(Pause.)

What

EMILY: Will you carry me to the car when my mom gets here?

JUSTIN: Really?

EMILY: Yeah, my joints swell up at night and I'm in so much pain right now. You can just carry me and then leave. I'm sorry.

JUSTIN: No, that's okay. Will your mom . . .

EMILY: What?

JUSTIN: If I carry you
Just that image

EMILY: It'll be fine
She loves you

JUSTIN: Sure.

EMILY: Thank you.

JUSTIN: Yup.

And uh . . . I do want to tell you something at some point

EMILY: What is it?
      Tell me now

(Kevin comes back and sits down.)

      J, just tell me now
JUSTIN: Kevin are you okay?
KEVIN: mhm.
EMILY: Okay, let's, let's say this for
JUSTIN: America?
EMILY: "Amurica"
JUSTIN: Why not
EMILY: Amurica! Why not. No you're right, it needs it. For Char-
      lottesville. And the nation at large. But also for my mother.
      The new president of this tiny little place.

(They each get out their rosaries.)

      Okay yeah I just need the words
JUSTIN: Yup
EMILY: Just some of the words
JUSTIN: The words are good
EMILY: In the name of the Father and of the Son and of the Holy
      Spirit.

         Our Father who art in Heaven,
         hallowed be thy name,
         Thy kingdom come,
         thy will be done,
         on Earth as it is in Heaven.

JUSTIN:

         Give us this day our daily bread,
         And forgive us our trespasses

as we forgive those who trespass against us
And lead us not into temptation,
but deliver us from evil.

Amen.

EMILY:

Hail Mary full of—

(Suddenly, Kevin vomits all over himself.)

KEVIN: Oh, damn
JUSTIN: Oh
EMILY: Oh gosh

(Kevin sobs. They watch him.)

KEVIN *(From the ground)*: please don't tell Teresa about this
this is not what I was given—I have chosen this—I have
chosen to destroy myself—

(He tries to blow his nose onto the pavement.)

Ah man my nose—it stings
It stings in my nose
Does this happen to you does it happen where your
nose, it goes in your nose
EMILY: Your nose
KEVIN: It went up in my nose too
Ow, oh, ow
It hurts in my nose
EMILY: I need to go to the bathroom
J, will you carry me?
JUSTIN: Yup.

(Justin lifts Emily up, and holds her like a bride in his arms. She's holding her cane.)

EMILY: Be back in a second, Kevin.
So sorry, I just really really need to go to the bathroom all of a sudden
Oof ow
Love ya.
KEVIN: Love
Mhm

(Justin carries Emily off.
Kevin lies on the ground and keeps sobbing. He tries to blow his nose onto the pavement. Slowly, he gets himself into sitting position. And slowly, he starts cleaning himself up. He uses his tie to wipe up the vomit, and then he bunches his tie up and puts it in his pocket.)

It stings so bad

(Eventually, Justin returns.)

Hey, I'm gonna um
Go back to the uh motel
JUSTIN: Are you okay to drive?
KEVIN: No yes I'm okay.
JUSTIN: Nah, you ain't.
KEVIN: Yes though. And
I'm so, so sorry about that crazy moment where I vomited.
I think I'm upset.
My nose is still

(Kevin is shivering. He tries to blow his nose onto the pavement.)

Man, my nose
>Has this ever happened to you with the nose
>When you throw up

JUSTIN: I haven't thrown up in like sixteen years

KEVIN: Haha

JUSTIN: Haha

KEVIN: Why am I shivering, why am I shivering so

JUSTIN: It's okay

KEVIN: I really want a girlfriend
>I drank that whiskey

JUSTIN: You can sleep on my couch

KEVIN: How do you do the thing where you *know?*

JUSTIN: I don't . . . What?

KEVIN: You have a way

JUSTIN: What way?

KEVIN: A, just, a, you have a

(He tries to show Justin with his hands.)

JUSTIN: There's nothing that I *know.* I've just mapped it all out in my head and I'm just hoping I'm right about it all. I think I am, but I don't know.

KEVIN: I'm awful.

JUSTIN: No.

KEVIN: Yes. Pathetic and
>At any moment, I feel this—I
>Justin, seriously, I think I'm in *love* with . . . I fall in love with SO MANY
>This college was the only thing keeping me from, just, dissolv
>Just watch, I'm gonna get cut loose—and I'm whipping over into the
>You know, The World
>And I might love it.

JUSTIN: This is the world.

KEVIN: No I mean the
> The
> You know
> And I might love it.

(Kevin lies down. Presses his forehead into the ground. He blows his nose onto the pavement.)

JUSTIN: I've been there. Before I decided to come back to school. I was *there*. I had a

(Pause.)

I was there for a while.

(Pause.)

There's nothing to love, really.

(Justin looks at Kevin, who has passed out.)

Kevin?

(He nudges Kevin. Kevin wakes up.)

KEVIN: Hey.

JUSTIN: Are you okay?

KEVIN: Let's make a fire.

JUSTIN: Too dry. Fire advisory.

KEVIN: I'm in love with Emily.

JUSTIN: What?

KEVIN: Yes—I want to take care of her.

JUSTIN: You need to stop this.

KEVIN: Stop what

JUSTIN: You need to stop this before you say something to Emily.

Hear me?

Hey, hear me?

I'm serious.

KEVIN: Why? Cuz you love her too.

JUSTIN: Stop, no. I just don't want you to overwhelm her. Or say the wrong thing.

She gets affected by people's emotions.

KEVIN: Uh-huh.

(Kevin spits onto the ground.)

JUSTIN: Hey, go take a nap inside.

KEVIN: You know, maybe I don't want to.

And maybe I want to protect her from *you.*

JUSTIN: What does that mean.

KEVIN: You know what it means.

JUSTIN: No I do not.

KEVIN: "No I do not." It means maybe I don't want you to do to her what you did to Teresa.

JUSTIN: Whoa

KEVIN: I always thought Dr. Gina was wrong to give you clemency. I don't know why she didn't tell President Robinson—he woulda kicked your ass to the curb. I just don't get why she protected you. Teresa made sense—it was her last semester and she was Dr. Gina's protégé. But you? You were just this old-ass freshman with tattoos and an ex-wife, and she let *you* stay?

(Justin stares Kevin down.)

I uh

Sorry.

JUSTIN: You know nothing about it. When I got here I was older than you are now. I'd made some serious mistakes. I was poisoned. This school was my antidote. And then when I poisoned myself again, Dr. Presson gave me a second chance, which saved my life. Do you have any idea of the grace . . .

(He takes a breath.)

And let me tell you, you slippery shit, if you don't clean your temple up, you are going to ruin a lot of lives before you ruin your own. You stink, dude. You stink like the devil.

(Kevin chuckles to himself. He lights up another cigarette. He looks at Justin.)

KEVIN: Cool. Goodnight.
JUSTIN: Goodnight.

(Kevin walks into the shadows. Justin tries to clean the blood from the porch again. Teresa comes outside.)

TERESA: Hey. Where'd you go?
JUSTIN: Had to check on Emily.
TERESA: So are you just like her knight in shining armor now?
JUSTIN: Nah she just needs someone to help.
TERESA: Oh please, she has got you wrapped around her finger. Can't even get five minutes alone with you.
JUSTIN: You were on the phone.
TERESA: I was beckoning you to stay.
JUSTIN: Was it Patrick?
TERESA: It was a quick call. I was waiting for you to come back in. And you didn't. So then I started dictating a new essay. Your song inspired me.
JUSTIN: Nuh-uh.

TERESA: Yeah-huh. The idea of "Nothing." Being a generation
that doesn't want to be a bunch of Nothing.

JUSTIN: Well I gotta check that out then.

TERESA: Do you read my site?

JUSTIN: Sometimes.

TERESA: Justin. I'm flattered.

JUSTIN: Well the writing's good.

TERESA: Hey, thank you.

JUSTIN: Yup.

How have you uh . . .

TERESA: Don't.

JUSTIN: What

TERESA: Just don't

JUSTIN: Don't what

TERESA: Don't melt me

JUSTIN: What do you mean

TERESA: You're trying to melt me

JUSTIN: Wasn't meaning to

(Kevin walks in from the shadows.)

KEVIN: Flirting y'all?—the *audacity*

TERESA *(Startled)*: Whoa

JUSTIN: We weren't. Jeez.

KEVIN: Teresa where'd you go for so long?

TERESA: I was recharging.

KEVIN: Look, it's the three of us, together again. Can you believe
it?

(Kevin gathers them into a group hug.)

TERESA: Kevin, there was never a "three of us."

KEVIN: Teresa I have a question for you.

TERESA: Okay

KEVIN: Can I have some of your cocaine please with all my heart

TERESA: Kevin, *what?*

KEVIN: No oops—

Real question is:

Y'all know I didn't tell her, right?

TERESA: Tell who?

(Unseen by Kevin, shielded by the group hug, Teresa starts gently caressing Justin's hand. He caresses hers back.)

KEVIN: Dr. Gina. You thought I did, but I didn't. I kept the promise.

TERESA: Kevin, I don't want to talk about this right now.

KEVIN: But that's why you hate me now, right? You think I snitched. But I didn't. I wouldn't have done that. You were my best friend. You were bigger than all of it, for me.

(Emily walks outside slowly. Justin rushes over to help.)

EMILY: Thank you J

TERESA: Kevin ask me a real question.

KEVIN: Oh a real question—ummmm YEAH

I'm really confused about why you think there's gonna be a war

And I want you to tell me

Because I want to be stronger

TERESA: No you don't

KEVIN: I do. I want to be stronger. I don't want to be subsumed by the invaders.

Please—tell me about the war. So that I can recognize it. So that I can fight.

TERESA: Okay. Look at you.

Okay, soy boy. Good.

Were you there when I was talking about the cycles?

KEVIN: What's a soy boy?

TERESA: Were you there when I was talking about the cycles?

KEVIN: The cycles? No.

TERESA: Basically we're all being called to be heroes because history goes in generational cycles and you can trace as far back as history goes.

KEVIN: What do you mean generational cycles?

TERESA: I'll explain.

JUSTIN: Is that from that book? I wanna read that.

TERESA: Yep.

KEVIN: What book?

TERESA: *The Fourth Turning.*

KEVIN: Oh—history repeating itself? That's just Plato. Timocracy becomes oligarchy becomes democracy becomes tyranny becomes timocracy becomes oligarchy becomes democracy becomes

EMILY: What are we talking about?

TERESA: They want me to explain why there's a war coming.

EMILY: Oh gosh

TERESA: Do you not want me to

EMILY: No it's okay

TERESA: Okay so

EMILY: Is this the Steve Bannon thing

TERESA: Yeah but

KEVIN: Bannon got axed last night! Did you see

TERESA: Of course I saw. He'll be back. And yes Emily, Bannon loves this theory, and so does Pat Buchanan

KEVIN: And also Plato

EMILY: My mom hosted a Pat Buchanan rally at our house when we were kids

TERESA: I know.

KEVIN: Whoa. Your mom

JUSTIN: That's diehard

EMILY: Is it

I don't know anything

TERESA: Pat Buchanan's insane. He's amazing.

EMILY: Is he

I don't know anything

TERESA: So there's four turnings. Each one of them is a couple of decades.

(She uses her hands a lot when she's explaining things.)

High.

Awakening.

Unraveling.

Crisis.

High awakening unraveling crisis.

High is a time of institutional security. And conformity. And the economy booms.

It's like. The fifties.

Awakening is when the institutions are questioned and attacked because people want to feel free again, they want to feel less stifled. So that's the sixties, the seventies. Hippies. Civil Rights. But also Vatican II, John Paul II. Spirituality, authenticity, you get it. It allows something tragic to happen like Roe v. Wade. It messes things up, plants the seeds for the crisis.

So then *Unraveling* is weird. It's like, we break into different camps. Institutions aren't trusted anymore, and there's a ton of emphasis on personal freedom—but more like, *license.* Things get a little decadent. People go off into their different camps. Culture wars. Eighties, nineties.

Then comes *Crisis.* That's the fourth turning. It's destruction, it's revolution, it's war. The nation almost doesn't survive. Great example is the Civil War, and the economic crisis before that. Or the Great Depression into World War II. And it's right now. The national identity crisis caused by

Obama. Liberals think it's Trump. It's the fight to save civilization. People start to collectivize and turn against each other. It seems like everything's ending—we're all gonna die. No one trusts each other. But the people who do trust each other form crazy bonds. Somehow we get through it, we rise from the ashes, and breach back into a High.

And those four turnings make a saeculum—

KEVIN: Saeculum?

EMILY: Saeculum

TERESA: Saeculum saeculum, like eighty–ninety years

KEVIN: Saeculum—take me to your saeculum

TERESA: Shut up Kevin

But within each of these turnings, there's an *archetype* that defines it.

Prophet.

Nomad.

Hero.

Artist.

Prophets are born near the end of a Crisis, at the beginning of a High. They grow up when shit is generally okay, during a High. They're a little self-indulgent, a little smug. But they become the wise elders during the Crisis. They're Baby Boomers.

Nomads are born during an Awakening, and they were alienated as children, and they don't have a strong sense of institutions and they're wanderers. So they're super pragmatic. And they're resilient after the Crisis.

Heroes are born during an Unraveling. They're team-oriented. They're optimistic. They're civically engaged. They fight bravely during the crisis. They're the generation that fought in World War II. And they're us. Right now.

EMILY: Wow I love that

KEVIN: What about Artists

TERESA: Oh right *Artists* are born during a Crisis. I don't really get, like, why they matter, but yeah, they're artists. But yeah *we're* all Heroes.

JUSTIN: What's the cutoff date?

TERESA: Justin, you were born in 1979?

JUSTIN: Yep.

TERESA: Oh, okay. You're cusp, but you're Nomad.

JUSTIN: Sounds about right.

KEVIN: But we're all heroes?

TERESA: Yep. Basically anyone who graduated high school after the year 2000.

JUSTIN: Dang yeah I was '97.

EMILY: Oh y'all, my parents were just talking about this at dinner. They were saying that they think our generation has a spiritual hunger, and like a bravery. And that they see it on both sides. Like both sides desperately want the good.

TERESA: Interesting

KEVIN *(Really has to pee)*: Heroes haha—that's so— Heroes— Can we— Like what is this a video game— My friend showed me a—VR— It friggin— Freaked me out—

(He runs off to pee.)

EMILY: And I just thought that was so beautiful because I really do know so many young people our age who are so good. Like all of us, as a generation. Including people who work for Planned Parenthood, Democrats, a drag queen I know . . . they're all good.

TERESA: Okay well
      I mean hmm I mean . . . I don't know about drag queens
      And Planned Parenthood are you *kidding*

EMILY: Yes she's my friend Olivia and she's really so wonderful

TERESA: This is the friend we were talking about in the tent, right?

EMILY: Yes and can we please not—

TERESA: Okay no, because every generation has the archetype but also plenty of people who are the explicit *antithesis* of the archetype

JUSTIN: Yeah I was gonna ask—

TERESA: Yeah! I mean if you're a hero, that implies a villain, right? I mean I don't know how I'm supposed to fall in line with a greater movement of heroes if they're supporting candidates who believe in late-term abortions. If candidates can't even look out for an unborn baby, I don't know how we can trust them with literally any other issue.

EMILY: But it's not the only issue

TERESA: It kind of is, actually.

EMILY: But people aren't *evil* who

TERESA: Maybe they are though.

EMILY: Teresa you're not listening—

TERESA: Fine, I'll shut up, I'll stop, this is the problem, no one knows how to debate, we literally can't hear each other.

(Kevin returns.)

KEVIN: I can hear everyone

TERESA: Oh yeah?

KEVIN: Yeah, what are we talking about? Can liberals be good— is that the argument?

TERESA: It's not just "liberals," we're talking about baby-killers.

KEVIN: Okay yeah—right right right

Yeah it's all about the woman's body

The woman's right to choose

TERESA: Yes we know that. But how can you "hear" that when the flip-side of the argument is that it's the murder of a child?

KEVIN: What

TERESA: Sorry I'm drunk what I mean is—how can you "hear" that when the FLIP-side of the argument is that it's the MURDER of a CHILD.

KEVIN: Oh I was just saying that

    I know what their argument is

    It's like: "Keep your hands off my body."

TERESA: We *are* keeping our hands off their bodies, that's the whole fucking point.

KEVIN: Okay well like!

    "It's my body, it's my choice."

    Those are just the words

TERESA: Murder is one of the things you're not allowed to choose.

KEVIN: No I mean bahhh

    I'm not arguing on their side

    I'm just saying what their side is

TERESA: I know, and I'm saying that their side is ignoring our side. Where we say it's murder.

KEVIN: But maybe they feel like our side is ignoring their side

TERESA: What exactly are we ignoring?

KEVIN: The part about the body like the Choice

TERESA: The choice to commit murder.

KEVIN: I guess they um

    I guess they . . .

    Right? they don't think it's murder?

    Literally guys I'm just devil's advocating

TERESA: See, I think their inability to address that question of whether it is or isn't murder—the fact that they sidestep that question completely—it implies their guilt. They do know it's murder.

    They do know it's murder.

    They just want to be allowed to do it.

EMILY: Oh man this is stressing me out

TERESA: I'm sorry and I'm sure your friends are nice and cool but they're part of a system that is evil.

    If your friend works for Planned Parenthood, she's not a good person.

EMILY: She is a good person. She's kind and altruistic and she's good.

TERESA: Look I do believe there are some people, because of the way they were raised or wanting to appear trendy, who call themselves pro-choice or use birth control or whatever and are more or less good in a general mediocre way. But to actually *work* for the epicenter of abortion in America? The place that *sells baby parts*? That takes calculation. You have to know what you're doing and do it anyway.

EMILY: She does know what she's doing. She believes in helping women. And she flat out does not think it's murder. And I thought the baby parts thing was a hoax.

TERESA: No it was proved, they proved it. The hoax thing was a hoax. Look it up.

EMILY: OKAY but at Planned Parenthood it's like . . . trying to provide safe access because people will always do it anyway unfortunately, and like, also, just as an *institution*, they're really more about services for women because that stuff is way underfunded, and it's like abortion is just one tiny part of the services they provide.

TERESA: "Murder is just one of the services we provide . . ."

EMILY: Can you stop talking to me like I don't know it's murder? I know it's murder. Do you know what my job was before I had to move here?

TERESA: I think I heard

KEVIN: Aid for Women

EMILY: I worked for Aid for Women.

TERESA: Okay and what is that

KEVIN: Pro-life thingy

EMILY: A pro-life women's advocacy organization in Chicago, which provides homes and communities and assistance to pregnant women with nowhere else to go. We helped domestic-abuse victims, refugees, homeless women choose *life*, against all odds.

TERESA: Right, and this is my point—

EMILY: But it's about these women, Teresa. These beautiful women, these strong women. They taught me so much about what it's *actually* like. And how hard these decisions actually are. And how the real problem is with men who abuse and rape and *systems*, *systems* that try to keep women down. The problem's not with the women who get an abortion because they don't know what else to do. Even if they do consider it the end of a life, they feel like they have no other choice, or they're afraid to bring it into the world and that makes so much sense. It's all so terrifying.

TERESA: For me, when I hear you say these things, I'm remembering articles about Holocaust victims, or uh, survivors, who had all this affection for these Nazi guards and doctors and all these anecdotes of kindness and, y'know, just because there are decent people trapped in an evil system, that doesn't make the system decent.

EMILY: What . . . ? I'm saying the system *isn't* decent . . .

TERESA: But okay, we shouldn't just *allow* the system to keep surviving because we like a few women. And it doesn't make the Nazi guards and doctors any less evil, just because they demonstrated some kindness . . .

EMILY: Why are you comparing this to Nazism? Olivia is not a Nazi.

TERESA: Well she's an agent of the modern-day Holocaust.

EMILY: It's not a holocaust. I believe that abortion is murder and I believe that there are horrible people who want to abort Down syndrome babies and all of these things, but I don't think it's the same as a holocaust . . . I just . . .

TERESA: Yes you do.

EMILY: No, it's different.

TERESA: How is it different? Because they're innocent fetuses? Okay, then it's worse than a holocaust.

EMILY: No it's not . . . it's not an organized effort to get rid of an entire race . . . it's . . .

TERESA: A holocaust is defined as slaughter on a mass scale.

EMILY: Okay so let's say it is a holocaust, okay, let's say that's true. Let's say the babies are the Holocaust victims—what does that make the *mothers*?

TERESA: They're the—

EMILY: Do not tell me they're the Nazis. Just don't. Do not.

TERESA: I wasn't going to. I just . . . mm. I think maybe some of the mothers are victims too. Look we don't need to break it down this way. It's not a one-to-one correlation.

EMILY: I just think you're not looking at it from the perspective of these *women*, Teresa—

TERESA: You're allowed to like your abortionist friend Olivia. But you're not allowed to tell me that she's equally as good as you. That the work you were doing in Chicago and the work she's doing in DC are equal. She's contributing to a genocide. A pogrom.

She's on the wrong side.

You're on the right side.

You are the good in this world, girl.

And you know it's true.

EMILY: Well I feel like all I'm asking for, all I'm ASKING for, is just a bigger dose of empathy—

TERESA: Oh don't with the *empathy*. Liberals are empathy addicts. Empathy empathy empathy. Empathy is *empty*. Hannah Arendt says we don't need to feel what someone else is feeling—first of all that's impossible, second of all it's self-righteous and breeds complacency, third of all it's politically irresponsible. Empathize with someone and suddenly you're erasing the boundaries of your own conscience, suddenly you're living under the tyranny of their desires. We need to know how to *think* how they're *thinking*. From a distance.

JUSTIN: Or try to *love* them.

TERESA: Sure yes.

EMILY: Beautiful, J.

TERESA: Yes yes very beautiful, but politically? It can't be about gooey feeling, it's thought—*thought*. Comprehending each other's thinking is the only possible political corrective, and we've almost completely lost the ability to do it. But I know how to do it. It's my job. And I *know* what your friend is thinking.

EMILY: Okay so what's she thinking?

TERESA: She's thinking: "Hi, okay, I'm Olivia, I'm such a good person for helping all these women, I'm so *great*, and you're about to get an abortion and *you're* so great, and we're *all* so great, and now let's go into this room and do this thing and your doctor is *so* great, and oh btw if you start to wonder if there's another presence here, someone small and silent with us, someone who could be just as great as us but will never have the chance, push that down, push it away, don't think about it, *we're* the great ones, here and now, because we say so."

EMILY: I'm sorry I just think that's incredibly reductive.

TERESA: She's essentially thinking in one of two modes: willful ignorance or knowing evil—

EMILY: Not evil no. Even if she's ignorant or blind I don't think she's evil.

TERESA: Sit her down with me for twenty minutes and watch her sweat—you might change your mind.

EMILY: You're very cocky.

TERESA: Thank you.

EMILY: You're not all-powerful, Teresa. Other people could make you flustered. J, do you want to . . .

JUSTIN: Shouldn't.

EMILY: Kevin, do you understand what I'm saying at all

KEVIN: I, um . . . sorta . . .

EMILY: I'm not good at debating, but I have some friends who, like . . . and I'd like to see that. There are people who are better at debating.

TERESA: No, you're in an excellent position to debate. You actually have real-world *experience*. You're *great*. I'm your biggest fan.

EMILY: No.

TERESA: Yes. Objectively. But I'm sorry, I can't subscribe to some kumbaya bullshit about everyone being good. Some people steal, some people cheat on their spouses, and they will be forgiven, blah blah blah. But some people murder babies. Fuck them. They don't get off.

EMILY: I don't know I don't know I don't know. It's a system. It's *nuanced*.

KEVIN: Can I ask—what is the *system*

EMILY: Men.

TERESA: It's the culture. It's the education. It's literally everything you see on TV.

KEVIN: Like what? The news?

TERESA: Ninety-nine percent of it. Mainstream media. And all the shows. All the movies.

KEVIN: But you watch TV you love all the shows

JUSTIN: They're

TERESA: What shows?

KEVIN: Don't you love, like . . . *Portlandia. BoJack Horseman.*

TERESA: I watch the shows they're entertaining but the shows do not determine my lifestyle.

EMILY: I love those shows.

JUSTIN: They're

EMILY: "Put a bird on it." Haha.

TERESA: Entertainment is inherently Dionysian, and that's a good thing in *moderation*. But it's become our national gospel.

JUSTIN: They're

KEVIN: Our president is an entertainer

TERESA: Do you want to talk about that? I could talk about that.

JUSTIN: It's

KEVIN: Plato predicted Trump

EMILY: No Trump please no Trump

KEVIN: Trump is Plato's "shadow-bleached rich man hung with superfluous fat, sitting in helpless confusion—"

JUSTIN: It's

TERESA: Trump is a Golem molded from the clay of mass media and he's come to save us all.

KEVIN: Damn

TERESA: And even if he himself is confused, he has the ability to spit out digestible soundbites rooted in decades of the work of the most brilliant conservative think tanks in the country.

JUSTIN: It's

EMILY: He's a gaseous barf bag and I pray for his soul

Okay y'all now Justin

You were gonna say something

JUSTIN: Oh nothing, the moment has passed

EMILY: No what J

What

JUSTIN: Are you okay

Is this all stressing you out

EMILY: No I'm okay

I just want everyone to love each other

TERESA: We love each other we love each other.

EMILY: I love you all so much I want to cry

Really, really

Everything is going to be okay and I love you all

I love you, I love you, I love you, I really do

KEVIN: We love you too, Emily

TERESA: We love you so much.

EMILY: Really?

TERESA: I mean . . . yeah.

EMILY: Okay, because you're fierce. It's great. I love you.

Justin what did you want to say?

JUSTIN: I wanted to say something about the liberal . . .

The nice young liberal people. And the system.

TERESA: Okay what.

JUSTIN: So these nice young liberal people are blinded by a system that distracts them from true moral questions and refocuses their attention onto fashionable and facile questions of identity and choice: which gender do you want to be today?, how much sex can you have today?, how many babies do you want?, and how do you want them to look?, which is really all part of a larger ideological system that is rooted in an evil, early twentieth-century quote unquote progressive trend towards quote unquote perfection, eugenics, and crypto-racism, endorsed by Margaret Sanger, an American eugenics system which persists, which wants to eliminate anything unclean or imperfect, including black babies and Down syndrome babies, and create a sterilized world based around state-mandated pleasure and narcissism. These are just facts, look it up y'all.

I can honestly say that, having lived in that world, and being a thirty-eight-year-old nomad, I can guarantee that ninety-nine percent of them are willing to just be led blindly into the cave, hooked up to a heroin drip of self-satisfied digital activism and committing vile acts of self-gratification because they're told that it's important to "experience" life, when actually they're numbing themselves to the possibility of real sacrifice or any chance of an ethical life, rooted in the grit and toil of suffering in the name of Christ.

And: there are more of them. We lost the popular vote, by a lot. Despite the indulgences afforded us by our wealthy backers and our electoral loopholes, we lack a unified youth movement. And they have that. And they're mobilizing. In many ways, they are in power. And they're trying to wipe us out. They're wishing for our death. And the only way to survive is to block them out, to focus on the Lord. Try to outlive them. Bake bread, make wine, work the earth, shelter wanderers, and survive.

TERESA: You talk like they're In Power. But they're not in power. We are.

JUSTIN: Maybe for now—

TERESA: No, and there are more of us, too. There are. We just aren't as loud, and we don't have control of the media. And we need to come together to *fight*, not to *bake bread*. It's honestly baffling to me that someone as strong as you would *already* be giving up the fight when it's barely begun—

KEVIN: Teresa Teresa

TERESA: What

KEVIN: I don't feel like a hero

TERESA: Okay

KEVIN: But the thing

I was born in 1989

I'm supposed to be a hero

TERESA: Well it's an archetype. Not everyone is a hero. It's just an archetype—a collective thing.

KEVIN: But I could be a hero. If I learned how to shoot a gun . . . I was always afraid of holding one cuz I thought I'd just stare into the barrel and pull the trigger.

EMILY: Kevin . . .

KEVIN: Haha sorry, but if there's a war coming, then uh I can be part of the heroes! I'll definitely die I'll definitely die. But I'll die with the heroes. You guys, Teresa is saying we're heroes! Let's be heroes! Come on let's be heroes. And hahaha okay here's my thing: if there's a war coming then why is Catholicism all about sex, seriously why is Catholicism OBSESSED with telling me not to have sex because all that led to is that I have an addiction to the internet and it's like I'm combing through it like an unholy un-Bible that keeps dissolving toxins into my eyes and all I ever think about is what to do with this goddamn thing between my legs—

JUSTIN: Kevin, can you stop.

KEVIN: Why

JUSTIN: You're scaring everyone.

KEVIN: Okay I didn't mean to scare everyone, I thought I was riffing—

    Was that not funny?

JUSTIN: No it was not. Talking about your genitalia in the company of women is not funny.

KEVIN: Well Justin at least my dick isn't covered in warts

TERESA: Whoa

JUSTIN: What did you just say?

EMILY *(Holding up her phone)*: Y'all my mom is here

    She wants to come say hi to everyone.

    Should I tell her not to

    I'm gonna tell her not to

KEVIN: Yeah we're too drunk

TERESA: No are you kidding? That's the only reason I'm here.

EMILY: Okay yeah

    I'll just say

    I'll just say "come say hi"

(Gina walks outside. Emily sees her and yelps.)

Oh, Mom I was about to text you

GINA: Hello everyone!

(Everyone suddenly shifts to their best behavior. Teresa rushes over to give Gina a hug.)

TERESA: Dr. Presson! Congratulations! Your speech today was so beautiful.

GINA: Oh Teresa thank you so much. You look beautiful. It really means the world to me that y'all came out

TERESA: We wouldn't have missed it

GINA: You're too much. Look at you—you're a real person!

TERESA: I am?

GINA: You are you are! And I heard you're betrothed! How are you sweetie?

TERESA: I'm well—I'm really—

GINA: Now, let me ask you a question.

Seven years out, tell me honestly, has the curriculum served you?

TERESA: Are you kidding, it was everything.

JUSTIN: Made me who I am today

KEVIN: The curriculum was AMAZING

Woop

(Kevin realizes he has vomit on his shirt, and tries to hide it with his hands.)

GINA: Kevin are you okay

KEVIN: Yes, yes I'm so good! Congratulations, Dr. Presson

You're going to be like the most amazing

Like the wonderful president of all

GINA: Thank you.

It was so lovely of y'all to come back for the ceremony.

Can you believe it—can you believe they chose *me*?

TERESA: Of course we can.

GINA: Well I thought they'd certainly appoint Jim. He's the brilliant one.

EMILY: Stop it, Mom.

GINA: Well he is, and anyway, he's the *man*.

TERESA: They made the right choice.

GINA: Well . . .

I think so too.

(She laughs. They all do.)

Where's everyone else?

EMILY: They went home, Mom, it's late

GINA: Oh wow, how did it get so late?

EMILY: You got drunk that's how

GINA: Well anyhow, thank you.

KEVIN: Our lives are so awful without TCW

GINA: Kevin why are you standing over there in the shadows

KEVIN: Because I've been bad tonight

Everyone hates me

TERESA: No we don't

EMILY *(To Gina)*: He's drunk

GINA: That's okay

Well, it was so nice to see everyone

Is anyone going to stick around for the eclipse?

EMILY: I think Kevin is.

KEVIN: Yes Kevin is! I can't wait. Everything's converging on

our school

The track of the umbra

The Path of Totality

GINA: That's right, and make sure you get those dark glasses—

KEVIN: Dr. Presson

GINA: Yes

KEVIN: Can you read that part of your speech

The part at the end

I need to seal it into my brain for like

The rest of my life

GINA: Oh, I don't have the speech with me

EMILY: I have it on my phone. You emailed it to me

GINA: Oh
I don't know
It's so late
KEVIN: Yes ma'am you're right
That's okay, sorry
EMILY: Mom just read it, everyone loved it
GINA: Out loud?
TERESA: Yes. Please.

(Gina laughs and looks at them.)

GINA: Okay I will
EMILY: Ginaaaa
Gia-ni-naaaa
Can't refuse the spotlight
GINA: Hush Emily

(Emily hands Gina her phone.)

KEVIN: Ah, thank you for doing this
Oh my gosh
GINA: This is so small.
How do I
Okay. Well, okay. Ahem.
"Our duty, our call as a college, is to behold—to bear witness—as Peter did upon the mountain (and think of that, climbing a mountain in that desert climate, breathless, thirsty, and then to see): Christ's transfiguration into brilliant light, a light that showed him the truth, sustained him through the martyrdom to come, a light that became ours, a light that daily pours down with morning fog from our Wind River Mountains, brightening our coursework, our wilderness adventures, and our mundanities. Meeting at that point where the frailty of human nature meets God,

where the time-weighted meets the eternal, we become ennobled to meet the world. Lit by an enduring radiance, we will make the essential freshness of our tradition appear. Students, climb joyously into our work here. Climb daily. We need you. We need you to serve as antidotes to those in the culture who drift into profligacy, whose vague tolerance slips so easily into indifference. We need you to be secure in moral persuasion, deeply sane, inventive, lucid, compassionate, and touched by divine fire. We pray that your example to the world will continue to 'flame out, like shining from shook foil.' Each of us knows our weakness, but at the edge of our nothingness is the abyss of God's kindness, that terrible beauty which sustains us."

(A breath.)

Is that good? Is that good, Jim's more of the writer—
KEVIN: It's beyond anything
JUSTIN: "Shining from shook foil"
GINA: That's Hopkins. Gerard Manley.
JUSTIN: I know
GINA: I know you know.
KEVIN: I know too.

> "The world is charged with the grandeur of God.
> It will flame out, like shining from shook foil,
> It gathers to a greatness, like—"

GINA: Thank you Kevin.
KEVIN: It's just beautiful. It's so beautiful.
GINA: Thank you Kevin.
TERESA: I love what you say about needing students who are deeply sane.

> Sanity is our scarcest national resource these days.
> I wish you were president when I was here.

GINA: But then I would have taught less.

TERESA: Never mind then.

KEVIN: DR. PRESSON?

GINA: Yes, Kevin? You don't need to yell. I'm right here.

KEVIN: Can I ask the dumbest

It's maybe the dumbest question I've ever asked but

Earlier people were like gathered around Teresa, who was doing her best impression of you

TERESA: What

EMILY: Not literally

KEVIN: No not *literally*, just

And we were, it got heated for a second, and suddenly I was like: wait.

Does this equal this? And why are you *conservative*

GINA: Pardon?

KEVIN: Just like

Why are *you* conservative

Independent of Catholicism

I mean Conservative, as a label

The party line

The uh, all the

I'm so . . . I don't know who to *be*, and

GINA: You're asking why Catholicism necessitates conservatism.

KEVIN: Yes ma'am.

GINA: Well, I think of Barry Goldwater's slogan: "In your heart, you know he's right."

(Teresa laughs a lot at this.)

I have that as a poster. It's hanging in my office.

TERESA: I remember!

GINA: I was a Goldwater Girl. So was Hillary Clinton. I stood with her on the same platform . . .

TERESA: Are you serious oh my gosh

GINA: I could have told you then that she had no spine.

KEVIN: NO BUT REALLY I was really asking

Not the slogan, the why

TERESA: Kevin, please

GINA: No, it's okay

KEVIN: All we know how to do is make things Catholic. That's all you taught us how to do. At other schools, they allow for different conclusions. But here, we're in the pursuit of the same conclusion—what you want isn't different conclusions, you want better poetry to get us to the same place. You chide us for not being imaginative, but you kick us out of school for smoking a joint. But there's a whole side to life that we're just pushing down. Like can't we be Catholic and not, uh . . .

TERESA: Kevin what are you talking about

GINA: No, shush Teresa

This is beautiful Kevin, you're so close . . .

Hm I want to answer

Hm, a little tipsy myself, Kevin, but let me try to . . .

Honey, of course we allow for different conclusions. But to focus on the conclusions is to miss the point. What we're after is the slow pursuit. The thrill of reason and rhetoric, prayer and poetry—a slow working out—taking apart the clock and putting it back together—hearing the music of its ticking with fresh ears and precise new understanding.

And God, let the understanding be slow.

Progressivism moves too fast and forces change and constricts liberty.

Gridlock is beautiful. In the delay is deliberation and true consensus. If you just railroad something through because you want it done, that's the passion of the mob. Delaying is the structure of the *republic*, which is structured differently in order to offset the dangers of democracy. I believe in slowness, gridlock.

The space between the cup and the lip.

Martin Diamond talked about this.

The little space between the cup and the lip.

Just waiting a little longer to taste the wine . . .

(She gestures as though she's drinking from a cup and holding it there still.)

You ever watch those old Hollywood romantic comedies that were made during the Hays Code era? Anything explicit would be censored. Working within that restraint, those movies are sexier than anything made today. A glance, a slight brushing against the hand, an innuendo . . . ah.

EMILY: Mom.

GINA: The difference between goal and form. For example, a man wooing a woman, right? The most "efficient" way to get her is to rape her . . . but the better way is the long process. The wooing.

EMILY: Mom, oh my gosh . . .

GINA: Or sorry . . . funerals!

The most efficient way is to burn the body, right away. But we don't. We have a ceremony.

All of the important things in life have this built-in delay. It gives form to things, it makes us citizens rather than subjects. And when things move too far in one direction, we pull it back. A gentle *return* to the original form. A *return* is wonderful. It's coming home.

KEVIN: I think that's really beautiful Dr. Presson, but you didn't answer my question.

GINA: What was the question?

KEVIN: Why do we have to be lumped in with . . .

Like, what do we do with Trump

GINA: That was not your question, dear.

KEVIN: It wasn't? Sorry, I thought it was.

GINA: I don't want to talk about Trump. Why is this that? Why are we making this that?

KEVIN: Because it is that, it very much is that. Trump talks about a return to the way it was, but he doesn't feel like coming home to me. He's gross, he's . . .

EMILY: He's so gross he's a gross monster

KEVIN: Yeah and all of us are dying inside because we're being equated with Trump, we're letting Trump exist—

TERESA: I'm not dying inside

KEVIN: And there's so much contradiction, Dr. Presson. Our Republican president is not *slow*. There's no space between the cup and lip. He drinks it all down. He rams things through.

GINA: He's a passing thing, a symptom. He's chemotherapy. I hope he gets impeached before he can re-campaign. I'm holding out for Pence.

JUSTIN: Amen.

GINA: Trump was made possible by the uneducated.

TERESA: I think some of his advisers are actually really smart—

GINA: No, they're not

They're adolescent

They're a symptom

TERESA *(Starting to pace)*: Adolescent? Okay. Symptom. Okay.

KEVIN: I love what you're saying, Dr. Presson. After I voted for Trump I vomited next to my car.

GINA: Yes, after I voted for him, I went to confession. And I'm *scared* of confession. I hate Trump. I hated Obama. But really, no one since Bush Senior had much regard for the Constitution. W. did a number on it too. What I will say is that there's danger from all sides.

JUSTIN: Yup

GINA: Liberty is being attacked, by both sides, and it's tragic to see. Polarities make way for a tyrant.

KEVIN: Did you just call him a tyrant?

GINA: Listen, FDR was the closest thing we had to a true dictator. He altered the shape of America in a debilitating way.
He started this pervasive *entitlement* mentality. A far more
necessary and dangerous quality of a dictator is skill as an
administrator and a bureaucrat. Which Trump does not
possess.

TERESA: Right. He's not a tyrant, he's strong. Because it's war.
America's at war. We're at war.

GINA: What is the war about?

TERESA: The fight for Western civilization. All it takes is one
big shift and we'll start to hear the gunshots, one at a time
and then more and more and more and more, getting
closer, they'll have a plan and we need to be ready, we need
to know what we'd die for.

GINA: Where are you getting this?

TERESA: From myself

GINA: You just made it all up?

TERESA: Well from the *news*, just look at the riots in—well, listen, from actually—
From Steve Bannon, he gave a beautiful talk at the Vatican

GINA: Oh, Bannon. Listen, I just don't trust any of these men—
they're all on their third wives.

KEVIN: They axed him last night. He's gone.

GINA: They did? I didn't see. Well, good.

TERESA: I'd love for you to watch his speeches, I can send you
the link. He said that one of the biggest open questions
in this country is whether the United States is willing to
embrace the strenuous life. "Is that grit still there, that
tenacity, that we've seen on the battlefields, fighting for
something greater than ourselves?"

JUSTIN: There's a quote by Teddy Roosevelt that's something like:
"When men fear work or fear righteous war, when women
fear motherhood, they tremble on the brink of doom."

KEVIN: I fear work

    I fear righteous war

    I'm trembling on the brink of doom

TERESA: And I fear motherhood, I've been infected by the culture . . . and that's part of the *problem*—

GINA: You fear motherhood?

KEVIN: I feel like a disease, Dr. Presson

GINA: What?

KEVIN: I feel like a disease.

GINA: What are you talking about?

EMILY: Actually, I'm the diseased one, Kevin

KEVIN: I'm so sorry.

GINA: What is going on here tonight?

    Why are you all so sad?

TERESA: I'm not sad

JUSTIN: Me neither

KEVIN: I don't know

TERESA: I'm so sorry about this, Dr. Presson

GINA: No it's okay

    This reminds me of Augustine's restlessness of the heart—*cor inquietus.*

    You're all forgetting your being.

KEVIN: What do you mean?

GINA: Oh, I don't know. Maybe I'm old, maybe I'm out of touch, maybe my conservatism isn't conservative anymore. Maybe it's more agrarian. And I'll be dead soon anyhow . . .

EMILY: Mom.

GINA: But in the meantime, I'm trying to *be.*

    Or your Heidegger? "Forgetfulness of being" is the biggest problem we face.

    To forget being means to forget how astonishing it is that anything exists at all.

    Aren't we allowed to just *be*?

Do we have to keep *making* ourselves? No. We already
are.

Climb a mountain. Make a meal. Behold creation and *be*.
Okay?

Anyhow. I'm hog tired.

JUSTIN: I can walk you to the car.

GINA: Okay, I'm going to the car

Let's go, Emily, come on

EMILY: Okay. One sec

TERESA *(Getting out her manuscript)*: So wonderful to see you,
Dr. Presson, and congratulations—

GINA: Thank you, Teresa. Write me a letter. Your hero Bannon—
thank God he's gone. He's crass, he's an identity-politics
toad. You're sounding a little silly. You need to look higher.

TERESA: I

What

EMILY: Too *harsh* Mom

GINA: Oh, she can take it.

TERESA: Dr. Presson

GINA: What is it Teresa

TERESA: I'm trying to

You taught me to try to form the body politic in the
image of . . .

In the true good, in the

GINA: I know

But you're getting it all wrong, sweetheart.

It disturbs me that you're aligning yourself with these
people.

These new people on the Right, they're not true conservatives. They're charlatans, they're hucksters. And honestly, darling, they're a bit racist.

TERESA: "Racist." Okay. I can't believe you just used that word.

Why did you use that word?

EMILY: Teresa, it's just true.

TERESA: I wasn't talking to you. Why'd you say that word to me, Dr. Presson?

GINA: Honey, I understand that the word is overused. But they're stoking the flames, it's not hard to see. It's not about race. It's about these nauseating movements, all that noise drowning out the discourse.

(Suddenly, the horrible screeching noise again. Everyone gasps and covers their ears.)

WHAT ON EARTH

JUSTIN: SORRY— GENERATOR
BE RIGHT BACK

(Justin rushes off. The sound dies down.)

EMILY: It's his generator, it's broken.

GINA: WOW—my heart is racing! WOO!

TERESA: Dr. Presson, aren't you a member of The John Birch Society?

GINA: Pardon? I used to be.

TERESA: And what was the society.

GINA: Why, are you trying to join?

TERESA: No, I'm just curious.

GINA: Okay. Well it was a network of concerned citizens, created in response to the New Deal—it was founded on George Washington's precedents, it was anti-collectivist, anti-communist—

TERESA: So you're anti-collectivist, and you look around today, what are the collectives that you see?

GINA: What is this, Teresa?

TERESA: What are the major movements, the major groups?

GINA: You're giving me an exam.

TERESA: Sorry, I . . .

GINA: No, let's have fun. Okay. Collectives. It would be Occupy Wall Street . . .

EMILY: That was like ten years ago, Mom—

GINA: Oh hush Emily no it wasn't . . . and it would be the Women's March, and Black Lives Matter.

TERESA: Right. And I would argue . . . The John Birch Society was formed in 1958. It wasn't in response to the New Deal. It was in response to the Civil Rights Movement.

GINA *(Laughing)*: No, Teresa . . . it was about Communism.

TERESA: No it was both—

GINA: Teresa, I was there. You weren't. The main target was Communism. Sure, there were a lot of Communists in the Civil Rights Movement. But it was about fighting unions. It was about entrepreneurs, small businessmen who didn't want to see the country fall prey to globalism, the agendas of—

TERESA: But all of these words are "codes," right?

(Justin comes back.)

GINA: Codes for what.

TERESA: For America's race problem.

GINA: What are you talking about?

TERESA: They're ways of talking about race. They're polite ways of talking about race. This is big on the Left right now and they're not going to back down from this.

GINA: Teresa what has happened to you? You sound like a pinko. Next you're gonna tell me we should be tearing down statues of Robert E. Lee.

TERESA: No of course not, I think that's a travesty, but I do think we need to change the ways in which our side talks about race. Their claim is not only that our political party is white supremacist, is ruled not only by racism, but by an economic need to have *slaves* under a different name—

GINA: Who is this in front of me? Who am I talking to?

TERESA: Black Lives Matter, the Women's March, BDS, Occupy—they're all together, they're "intersectional." They're united in the attempt to constantly lean on America's original sin—slavery. They're using that original sin to take over, and create a new America which doesn't resemble a true democracy at all, and which oppresses us in the same ways our ancestors oppressed them. As revenge. Literal revenge. So what do we do with that? We can know in our hearts that we're not racist, we can know that we're not looking to keep slavery alive, but there's no convincing them. So what are our choices? If we don't collectivize *ourselves*, we're going to be exterminated.

GINA: Collectivize ourselves? We have no need to collectivize. George Washington would be rolling over in his grave to hear you say this. And: we have the Constitution, dear.

TERESA: They *hate* the Constitution. They want to get rid of it. They think it's a white supremacist document designed to protect white men.

GINA: So *what*? Gather our torches and drive our cars into crowds? That's not helping our case.

TERESA: No, that's madness, but if we don't do *anything* . . .

GINA: What's all this "we." "We, we, we." Listen, every American heart needs to be *educated* in the *natural good*.

TERESA: Or what about Pat Buchanan?

GINA: What *about* him?

TERESA: Emily said you hosted a rally for him in the nineties.

EMILY: Sorry, Mom

TERESA: Why'd you do that?

GINA: Because I supported him for president.

TERESA: Why?

GINA: Because he was pro-life, an educated man . . .

TERESA: He was an incredibly controversial figure, you must have known that . . .

GINA: I'm not afraid of a little controversy.

TERESA: But you're ignoring the effect he had on the discourse.

GINA: I'm not ignoring anything—

TERESA: There were other conservatives you could have aligned yourself with. George Will or William F. Buckley. Or *Bob Dole*. But you didn't. Why?

GINA: They weren't as sure of where they stood.

TERESA: Because they weren't tough enough for you?

GINA: Maybe so.

TERESA: Tough about what?

GINA: About *life*, Teresa. You have to understand. And Kevin, this goes back to your question, too. When Roe v. Wade happened, we Catholics thought we had lost everything. We endured over forty years of moral degradation as millions of babies were aborted—it took strength, and patience. We had to cultivate that strength and prepare the younger generation to take up the fight in case we died before we won it and now we're finally finally taking the Supreme Court back. And to do that, we had to make com-promises. We had to create a voting bloc. We had to align ourselves with people whose priority was . . . ah.

TERESA: People whose priority was what? Own it.

GINA: Your tone, Teresa.

TERESA: I'm sorry. But you just used the word "we" like ten times.

GINA: I'm tired. I need to go to sleep. We're not on the brink of doom, okay?

TERESA: Dr. Presson, you told me that we *were*. Over and over and over again, in your courses—in Thucydides, Herodo-tus—you would bring it back to today. You would warn us about *today*.

GINA: Of course. There are Catholics being martyred around the world every day. Our *faith* will always be under threat of exterm—

TERESA: Pat Buchanan was a—

GINA: Don't interrupt me.

TERESA: Sorry.

GINA: Go ahead.

TERESA: No, you go.

GINA: No, I lost it. Speak.

TERESA: Pat Buchanan was a populist willing to say things that other people weren't. About how unmitigated immigration is leading to the erasure of White European culture in this country. About how black movements are funded by proven communists. About how there is a documented, daily, open attack on white Christians. And we're not allowed to talk about it. White people are the only people in the United States who aren't allowed to take public pride in who they are—

GINA: Okay, I see. I'm familiar with that anxiety, but beyond our tribal instincts, we need to be able to *compromise*, and we do that by appealing to the natural good . . .

TERESA: Okay, but that's what I've been *trying* to do, so what does that MEAN?!

GINA: It means CALM DOWN!

TERESA: I agree, okay? I agree. Everyone needs to calm down. But they're never going to listen to you, because you're *white* you're *white* you're *white*. We're all *white*. And our *white* language is the *white* language of the *white* oppressor.

GINA: Good Lord.

TERESA: Right? I know! Telling them to "calm down" is "a violence." It's a "microaggression."

GINA: Honey, none of this is news to me. What's bizarre is that you assume the only way to beat them is to play their game. Look, it's not their fault that they get manipulated by socialists, whipped up into these frenzies. If it takes more time for them to be satisfied, to realize that they're *fine*, that they're citizens now just like the rest of us, then so be it. They already got a president of the nation. I'm a

woman and I get to be president of this college. This was
all unthinkable when I was younger. To think in the terms
you're thinking in—it's limiting *their* liberty. It's lumping
us into groups based on our skin color rather than our reason. I believe in looking past skin color. I believe in hard
work. I believe in—

TERESA: Every thinker on the Left today would absolutely
decimate you. You're a little protected out here, you don't
have to deal with the protests and the pronouns and the
canceling and the . . . I just feel like you need to experience
the front lines. They'd look at you and point to how all
of your conferences are funded by the Koch Brothers
and they'd itemize the worst-hits of Trump's rhetoric
and call you *complicit*, and they'd point to your support of
Goldwater and his refusal to vote for the Civil Rights
Act—

GINA: He was a constitutionalist, he was trying to protect states
from federal overreach—

TERESA: It doesn't matter. History doesn't matter anymore.
Truth doesn't matter anymore. They want it gone. It hurts
their feelings. Why'd you host Pat Buchanan in your *home*
if you were just *compromising*?

GINA: Because I thought he could WIN. And I was wrong,
because he wasn't stupid enough to appeal to the masses.
On the issue of life, Catholics are called to be single-issue
voters, and I thought Buchanan had the abil—

TERESA: But your single issue isn't really being pro-life. Not
really.

GINA: What is it then? Enlighten me.

TERESA: It's Western Civilization. Which only survives by being
pro-life.

GINA: Teresa, that's absurd. I put my body on the line. I had
eight C-sections. After the *first*, every single doctor told

me to tie my tubes, to stop having children, that it would kill me. But I kept having them. I didn't do that for white Western Civilization, I did that for God.

TERESA: I hear you, and I think you're an absolute hero. Truly.

GINA: So, then, honey, if you're able to tell me in a polite and measured tone: what *exactly* are you proposing?

TERESA: *Not* being measured. *Not* being polite. I don't want to be polite anymore. We can't lie to ourselves. We're past that. We're in Crisis. They're coming for our tabernacle. They want to burn it down. They want to destroy the legacy of heroes like you. So I propose leveling up. I propose looking at the truth in the face. Knowing what it looks like. Knowing what we look like to them. It's not going anywhere. I propose not taking any *shit*. Not ignoring all the hypocritical *bullshit*. Going blow for blow. And being ready for the war, if it happens. *When* it happens. You call us racist, we'll call *you* racist. You call us white, we'll call you black. You call us Nazis, we'll call you abortionists and eugenicists. You call us ignorant Christians, we'll call you spineless hedonistic soulless bloviating bloodbags. But you stop doing that, and give this thing space and time to work itself out, we'll stop too. You focus your efforts on making this a better nation, an American nation, a republic of ideas, we will too.

GINA: Uh-huh. I see.

. . .

Where did I go wrong?

TERESA: You just lost track of the new thinkers.

GINA: No, Teresa. I failed you. This is a brutal and stupid way of thinking. Wrapped up in *identity*.

You're just as fragile as they are. Maybe more so. You're being ruled by *emotion*.

It's embarrassing. It's imbecilic. It's Un-Christian. I thought I was cultivating students of *character*. I thought our students were happy and strong. Was I wrong? Look at you, you're worldly, you're crude, and you're *weak*.

You're *one of them*.

TERESA: No, I'm not one of them. What? Listen, I have to deal with them every day, and by their standards, Bannon and Company are not the only racists. You are too. We all are. And I'm sorry if this rhetoric offends you, but—

GINA: It doesn't *offend* me, dear. You—*you*—have *disappointed* me. And it's heartbreaking.

You've managed to do it again, Teresa. You've managed to break my heart.

I risked my good standing at this school to give you clemency in your senior year. Now I wonder if I was wrong to ever treat you with gentleness.

You've reverted back to an emotional, fire-spewing slut. You're whoring yourself to popular opinion.

I do not recognize you.

And I despise the world you're trying to create.

(Pause.)

EMILY: Mother. I think you should leave.

GINA: Yes I *know*, Emily. Folks, I need to go sleep.

JUSTIN: See you on Monday, Dr. Presson. We've got new horses, you should come see them.

GINA: Okay. Are they trained?

JUSTIN: I'm working on it.

GINA: Great. I don't know how you get on those horses. Terrifies me.

JUSTIN: Copy that.

(Gina starts to exit. Justin blocks her path.)

One thing I've been wondering, Dr. Presson, is whether you'd consider doing marksmanship training for the students. I'd be happy to take on those courses, in addition to the horseback . . .

GINA: What? No, absolutely not. I don't want guns around the students.

JUSTIN: I'd make sure everything was as safe as possible.

GINA: *Why* are you asking me this *now*? I need to *sleep*.

JUSTIN: One of the things I love about this school is the way it hearkens back to the Ancient Greek model, in which students learned rhetoric, mathematics, metaphysics, but also trained in the art of war.

GINA: War war war, what's all this *war*?

JUSTIN: Ma'am, I believe Teresa is correct about the coming war.

GINA: Oh, Justin. Is this some sort of . . . gesture?

JUSTIN: Ma'am?

GINA: You're performing some kind of gesture for poor Teresa.

JUSTIN: I'm performing no kind of gesture, ma'am, just expressing my opinion.

GINA: Uh-huh. You know, you don't owe her anything, Justin.

JUSTIN: Ma'am?

GINA: Forget it. Look, we *cannot* appear to be some radical far-Right militant school.

JUSTIN: Yes ma'am but in an increasingly violent world—

GINA: I just don't want guns on campus, okay? I just don't like guns. And maybe that's me being *emotional*, but that's just how it is.

JUSTIN: Copy that.

GINA: Goodnight, Justin. And don't worry. Teresa will be gone tomorrow and then you can get your good sense back.

EMILY: Mother—leave.

GINA: Goodnight, Kevin. Go home.

KEVIN: Sssure

GINA: And Kevin?

KEVIN: Yes! Goodbye. Congratulations. Again it was a beautiful speech.

GINA: Thank you. Come visit me before you leave. We have an opening—we need a Dean of Admissions.

KEVIN: Oh wow

GINA: Consider interviewing? I think you'd be perfect

KEVIN: Are you serious?

GINA: I am.

You're close to something, Kevin.

KEVIN: Thank you so much, that would be . . . oh man, I'm really thinking about this

GINA: Good—come visit me.

Okay, night y'all.

And I'm sorry if I was a bit stern just now, Teresa. I love you, honey, but in the thin thin space between your intellect and your animal nature is the tiny cave meant for the Holy Spirit. For gut goodness. For grace. You've sealed it shut. You're turning your fear of motherhood into false machismo. Don't invent a war just because you're afraid to give your own body away to something higher. It was hard for me to admit this when I was your age, too, but real strength is in bearing a child—and then staying open to as many as God wants to give you.

And everyone:

Don't be dark and complicated, even though it's very Catholic. Strive for *peace*.

(Gina almost succeeds at leaving.)

TERESA: Dr. Presson! . . .

GINA: Teresa, I'm going to sleep.

TERESA: Yes, I just . . . I'm writing a book, my collected essays . . . I don't know if you heard, but I have a real following online and um . . .

I don't know if you've read any of them, but . . .

I was wondering if you wanted to write a blurb. I was going to ask you to write a blurb.

(Teresa gets a manuscript out of her purse. She holds it out toward Gina.)

GINA: Oh gosh I don't want all that paper. Can you send me the pdf?

EMILY: Mom just take it.

(Gina takes it.)

GINA: I don't like that website you write for.

TERESA: Right. Okay. Sorry.

GINA: No, it's okay. I'll read it when work calms down. I don't know if you heard but I got a new job recently.

TERESA *(Near tears)*: I know. Sorry.

Oh and I forgot to tell you . . .

I live right near the place where the Battle of Brooklyn happened . . .

Where, um . . . George Washington

(Pause.)

GINA: Okay. Thank you for telling me.

Come on Emily

EMILY: One second Mom, I

I think I'll get a ride home with Justin, if that's okay?

GINA: Is that okay with him?

JUSTIN: 'Course.

GINA: No, come with me now.

EMILY: Mother, no . . . I want to stay.

Please.

GINA: She sends me twenty-five texts about how she's desperate to leave, and then I rush over and it's "oh, never mind." And then you wonder why we have questions about this disease.

EMILY: Mother. You did not rush over. And I am out of bed for the first time in months. This is a cause for celebration and can I please just have your support.

GINA: Fine. Okay. You have my support. But then what did I come here for?

EMILY: To
      To see everyone
      They wanted to see you

GINA: Right.
      Congratulations to me.
      Well, whatever.
      Goodnight.

(Gina leaves.)

EMILY: Oh she makes me so mad. She's ridiculous, she's on a power trip. She's constantly trying to fix people, she's never meeting them where they are. She's constantly just focusing on what they're not. Ahh, I'm sorry y'all. But she's also a hero. I mean seriously, after all those C-sections, she survived breast cancer. And taught full-time the whole time. And she's got basically paper for knees and she's walking around in tremendous pain every freaking day. And she never complains. That's some faith. That's some faith. So y'all I guess we can forgive her for being a little intense.

KEVIN: She's not intense.

EMILY: Yeah, she said you'd be the Dean of Admissions.

KEVIN: Yeah, that's true. That was . . . yeah. Okay this . . . this is amazing. Guys I'm gonna come back to Wyoming maybe oh my God. Justin we can be roommates hahaha. No but

seriously—I gotta nail that interview. I need a new shirt.
Does the Walmart in Riverton have nice shirts?

(Teresa snorts.)

What, Teresa?

TERESA: Nothing. I just think you'd obviously be a horrible
Dean of Admissions.

(She laughs. Emily and Justin chuckle too.)

I heard you puke earlier.

KEVIN: Okay—okay—okay

    Yeah, Kevin—just take the joke—haha

TERESA: Hey wanna know what a soy boy is? It's a whiny bitch
trapped in the body of a man.

EMILY: Okay . . . wow. Maybe it's time for everyone to go to bed.

(Kevin starts hitting his leg, or something else scary.)

JUSTIN: Kevin, seriously, go to sleep.

KEVIN: Oh my God, stop trying to brush me under the rug
Justin

JUSTIN: What?

KEVIN: You keep trying to hide me

JUSTIN: No I don't

KEVIN: Yes you do

    You hate how weak I am

    You all hate how weak I am

    But in the next kingdom, my weakness will invert, and
I'll be as strong there as I was weak here. And you'll be the
weakest creature, Justin. You'll stink like the devil. You're
gonna burn in hell motherfucker, I'm gonna fuck you in
hell—

JUSTIN: KEVIN.
KEVIN: WHAT, JUSTIN
JUSTIN: STOP IT. RIGHT NOW.
KEVIN: STOP WHAT
    JESUS

(Justin moves toward Kevin, who runs toward Emily and falls at her feet.)

I'm going to split myself open
EMILY: Oh my Lord
    Kev what is wrong
    I've never seen you like this
KEVIN: Never yeah
    I hid it from you

(Kevin starts crying.)

I'm so drunk y'all
    I'm the drunkest I've ever been
    Oh and
    Emily
    For so long
    For so long I've wanted
    To bathe you, to bathe you, uh
JUSTIN: Kevin, that's it—
KEVIN *(Moving toward Teresa)*: And Teresa
    For so long
    For so long I've wanted you
    Wanted you to be my girlfriend
    For you to beat me up and teach me how to fuck
    When you told me you had sex with Just—

(Teresa pushes Kevin's face, hard, and his neck snaps back and he flips to the ground and lies there, maybe unconscious.)

TERESA: Oh my God
EMILY: Oh my Gosh
    Oh no

(Justin checks on Kevin.)

KEVIN *(Quiet)*: Damn Teresa

(Kevin snores.)

JUSTIN: He's okay
    He's snoring
EMILY: That could be bad though
    It could be a concussion right
    We should wake him up

(Justin goes to touch him and Kevin bolts awake.)

KEVIN: No I'm okay
    I'm so sorry Emily
EMILY: For what
KEVIN: For me
EMILY: For you?
KEVIN: For all of this night
EMILY: Why are you apologizing to *me*
KEVIN: This just shouldn't be anything that you have to see
EMILY: Kevin I'm fine, I'm here just like you
    Don't talk to me like I'm some pure

(Teresa starts approaching Kevin.)

TERESA: Oh my God
    I can't believe I
KEVIN: I'm sorry Emily

EMILY: Stop it

KEVIN: Sorry

TERESA: Kevin

Oh God

(Teresa goes to the ground and holds Kevin.)

I'm so sorry

KEVIN: I'm so sorry

TERESA: I'm so sorry

KEVIN: Are you holding me

TERESA: Yes

KEVIN: Why

TERESA: Cuz

KEVIN: I'm sorry

TERESA: I didn't mean to hurt you

KEVIN: I'm so sorry

You're holding me

TERESA: Yes

(Kevin lets himself be held for a moment, but then something strange happens. He can't bear it. He doesn't let himself be held. He gets to his feet.)

Are you okay? I'm sorry.

KEVIN: I'm fine. Sorry again. I'm fine and I'm sorry. Justin can I sleep on your couch?

JUSTIN: Sure

KEVIN: Thanks. Okay goodnight everyone. I'm fine.

Oh Teresa, uh . . . for a second I saw the mountain

TERESA: You saw the mountain?

KEVIN: For a second I fell asleep and I saw the mountain

TERESA: What mountain

KEVIN: Pingora Peak. The one we all climbed when we were freshman right? That one with all the burned trees cuz of the fire. We were camped out and sleeping. I was outside peeing. Then I saw someone coming down. From higher up the mountain. Carrying the stones. I couldn't tell if it was a he or a she—it wasn't either, it was more than one being in one being. They were carrying the stones. The stones had words on them for everything we've been missing. There are things we've been missing. Secret sacraments, forgotten commandments, right? And they were carrying the stones right down to where we were. And I wanted to wake you all up but I couldn't move. And then they walked right by me, inches away, and I could have reached out and touched them, but I didn't. They just kept moving. And I went back into my tent and fell asleep. And I never told anyone. Sorry. Goodnight y'all. I'm fine.

(Kevin leaves.
Teresa and Emily look at Justin.
The screech of the generator again.)

EMILY: OH GOD
TERESA: YOU HAVE TO FIX THAT

(It screeches and screeches.)

IS IT GOING TO STOP
EMILY: AHHHHHHH
TERESA: JUSTIN WHAT THE HELL IS—

(The screeching stops.)

WRONG WITH THIS PLACE
　　Oh okay
　　Well . . .

(She looks at Emily.)

Hey uh. Oh man, I just got really scared . . .

EMILY: Oh my gosh. Me too. Are you okay?

TERESA: Yeah I just

EMILY: I'm sorry about Kevin

TERESA: No that's whatever

EMILY: I'm sorry about my mom.

TERESA: No that was fun. No.

EMILY: What are you scared of?

TERESA *(Cold)*: Mm.

That my, mm.

That my wedding won't be beautiful. That it just won't be beautiful. That people won't know how to celebrate me, or my love.

(She gets quieter.)

Or just that people don't know me, that I don't let them know me

That I'm too private with my love

Or that I don't really know how to love at all

(Pause.)

JUSTIN: No, it'll be beautiful.

(Teresa frowns.)

TERESA: Thanks, Justin.

Okay. Goodnight.

Emily, tell your mom, uh . . .

Well, goodnight.

(Teresa leaves.

Now Emily doubles over in pain.)

JUSTIN: Hey hey

You okay?

(He helps her to a chair.)

EMILY: Lot of pain.
JUSTIN: Where
EMILY: Everywhere
JUSTIN: How long
EMILY: For like twenty minutes
JUSTIN: Why didn't you say something
EMILY: Everyone was trying to figure their things out
JUSTIN: You should have told me
     Breathe

(She breathes.)

EMILY: Oh my Gosh
JUSTIN: You're okay
EMILY: What did you want to say to me?
JUSTIN: We don't have to talk about that now.
EMILY: Tell me, I want to hear, that's why I stayed.
JUSTIN: Uh
EMILY: Please
JUSTIN: Okay well

(Pause.)

I think, I've been thinking . . . and I think I'm going to
enter the monastery
     The one in Abruzzo
EMILY: oh

(Pause.)

when
JUSTIN: End of the month.
     I'm gearing up to tell your parents sometime this week.

(Pause.)

I've prayed on it quite a bit and I think it's what's best
EMILY: I'm happy for you really J

(Pause.)

JUSTIN: I don't want you to feel abandoned
EMILY: I don't feel abandoned
        I'm just going to miss you
        You're so good to me and you're my best friend
        And I think you'd be such a good father that's all
JUSTIN: A father
EMILY: I just had a dream I had a vision of you as a dad
        But it's okay, I've been wrong before

(Pause.)

Is it really what you want?
JUSTIN: I was starting to feel a lot of anger and I don't know why
        And then a terrible compassion
        And then this terrible compassion
        And then paralysis . . .
        I'll just be a monk in Italy
        I'll just work the good small ways and pray for you and
EMILY: I need a buddy, J
        I really need one so bad
        Stay here

*(Far off, a gun goes off. Justin looks toward the sound. He turns
back toward Emily.)*

Just stay.

(More gunshots in the distance.)

JUSTIN: Uh I've been telling a lie all night.

EMILY: What? What lie?

JUSTIN: About the noise, the generator.

EMILY: What?

JUSTIN: When I first moved into this house, I felt the most horrible presence. It was suffocating me.

I had the house blessed. Father Paul came and basically scrubbed it down with holy water.

It didn't help.

And that screech you heard, it isn't the generator.

I don't know what that is.

(This hits Emily hard. She shakes her head. She laughs to herself.)

EMILY: I told a lie tonight too.

JUSTIN: Really?

EMILY: Yeah. It wasn't me this morning. It wasn't me lying there, saying f-this to God. I lied. It was this woman Tiffany—this pregnant woman I counseled in Chicago who ended up getting an abortion anyway, it was probably the worst session I had out of all of them. She was so mean to me, just like screaming at me and calling me a little white girl, a self-righteous c-word and all this horrible stuff, but it wasn't her fault, she had been hurt so much, I think really hurt, and she was this black woman who was desperate and so wounded and angry, and so I was lying there and I was convinced that I was *her*—I was in insane pain, on my bed, I couldn't move, and I was *Tiffany*, in Chicago, waking up so exhausted, and I had so much to do, and my brain was knives. I wasn't me.

(She curls into herself.)

JUSTIN: Buddy
      Buddy
EMILY: Don't call me that
      I hate myself
JUSTIN: Don't say that
      Hey
EMILY: I hate myself
JUSTIN: Emily
EMILY: No I don't, okay
      I don't then
      Why do I have a body?
JUSTIN: What—
EMILY: I'm just so tired of talking. There's nothing to figure out. We just eat each other up and die one by one. And in Heaven it's going to be so different, all the words and meaning will fade into no words and no meaning, just God everywhere through us all the time, and it'll hurt so bad. It'll hurt forever. You know? Ah fuckitfuckitfuckitfuckit fuck you, get out of here. Get the fuck out of here. Fancy fucking pity. Fuck your pity and fuck your empathy you self-righteous cunt. There's nothing there. Get the fuck out from behind that desk telling me what you think you know about me. I came in here thinking you would help me, the fuck was I thinking, you're a little girl. You don't know anything about me and fuck you. You can think of me but you cannot feel me. You cannot feel me. You cannot possibly ever feel what this feels like. High up in your tower of see-everything. You can't go back to the shit that became my shit, the knife that cut me. You can't fuse with me. You can't merge with me. And my pain doesn't make me better fuck you. And my pain doesn't bring me closer to Jesus fuck you. And fuck if-you're-feeling-it-you're-one-of-the-lucky-ones—fuck your holy fool, fuck your war, fuck your gridlock, fuck your Path of Totality, fuck your clemency,

fuck your grateful acre, fuck your grateful acre, the acre is not grateful, the acre is in pain, the acre is dying, your faith isn't full, your faith is empty, your faith is stupid, there's no one there, there's no one there and he hates you. Listen to me. I'm one of the damned, I'm the trampled-on, I'm the shit-covered, I'm the rotting, I'm the teeming mass, I'm the hacking cough, I'm the phlegm, I'm the vomit, I'm the bloody piss, I'm the look-away, I'm the shake-your-head, I'm the praying-for, I'm the prayer, I'm the oh no. You don't feel this, you can't feel this. And grace doesn't happen. It doesn't exist. The big bitch shits on your fuck. You don't know how dangerous this is. It's too dangerous, don't try to feel this, it'll kill you, it won't solve anything, leave me to die, get away from here. Help me oh God. Get me out of this. Get me to the water. Turn it off. The song is over. And I'm still here? And I'm just me? And I'm just me and I'm still here. I'm dead and look what I can do. Kill more on my way through. Feel it kicking. Know that it's in me and still kill it. Know that it's living and still kill it. Cut it out. Throw it away. Toss it out. Look away. Sign the paper. Walk around. Go to sleep. Wake up. A little later I'll let somebody else in. Then I'll fuck somebody else. Then somebody else. Then somebody else.

(She breathes. She realizes that she is standing. How did she get here? Justin is collapsed on the porch, right where he started the day with the deer. He can't look at her.)

JUSTIN: Emily, are you—what do I do
EMILY: What happened
JUSTIN: How do I help
EMILY: You don't have to help
JUSTIN: I didn't know
EMILY: You do know

JUSTIN: I didn't really know

EMILY: Know what

JUSTIN: The pain

EMILY: It's okay

     I love pain

     I love it

     I love pain

     We love it

JUSTIN: Emily—

EMILY: Ah okay. Okay. Guess what? I feel a little better now.

     Doopy-doo.

     Come on. We're okay.

     Doopy-doo.

     Doopy-doo.

JUSTIN: Doopy-doo.

     Yup.

EMILY: Simple as a doopy-doo.

JUSTIN: Just a simple hoopy-hoo.

EMILY: Yuppy-yoo.

THE END

WILL ARBERY is a playwright from Texas + Wyoming + seven sisters. *Heroes of the Fourth Turning* premiered at Playwrights Horizons in Fall 2019 and was a finalist for the 2020 Pulitzer Prize for Drama. It won the 2020 Obie Award for Playwriting, the Lucille Lortel Award for Outstanding Play, the New York Drama Critics' Circle Award for Best Play, and the Outer Critics Circle John Gassner Playwriting Award. Arbery also won the Whiting Award for Drama in 2020. Other plays include *Corsicana* (Playwrights Horizons), *Evanston Salt Costs Climbing* (The New Group), *Plano* (Clubbed Thumb), and *Wheelchair* (3 Hole Press). He's currently under commission from Playwrights Horizons, Manhattan Theatre Club, and Audible. He's a member/alum of New Dramatists, The Working Farm at SPACE on Ryder Farm, Interstate 73, Colt Coeur, Youngblood, and Clubbed Thumb's Early Career Writers Group. His plays have been developed at Clubbed Thumb, Playwrights Horizons, The Public Theater, New York Theatre Workshop, the Vineyard Theater, SPACE on Ryder Farm, Ojai Playwrights Conference, The Cape Cod Theatre Project, The New Group, EST/Youngblood, The Bushwick Starr, Alliance/Kendeda, and Tofte Lake Center. TV: HBO's *Succession* and *Irma Vep*.